MANAGING CREATION

Wiley Series On
ORGANIZATIONAL
ASSESSMENT AND CHANGE

Series Editors:
Edward E. Lawler III and
Stanley E. Seashore

MANAGING CREATION
The Challenge of Building a New Organization

DENNIS N. T. PERKINS
School of Organization and Management
and Department of Psychology
Yale University
New Haven, Connecticut

VERONICA F. NIEVA
Westat, Incorporated
Rockville, Maryland

EDWARD E. LAWLER III
School of Business Administration
University of Southern California
Los Angeles, California

A WILEY-INTERSCIENCE PUBLICATION

JOHN WILEY & SONS
New York   Chichester   Brisbane   Toronto   Singapore

This publication is designed to provide accurate and
authoritative information in regard to the subject
matter covered. It is sold with the understanding that
the publisher is not engaged in rendering legal, accounting,
or other professional service. If legal advice or other
expert assistance is required, the services of a competent
professional person should be sought. *From a Declaration
of Principles jointly adopted by a Committee of the
American Bar Association and a Committee of Publishers.*

Library of Congress Cataloging in Publication Data:

Perkins, Dennis N. T., 1942–
   Managing creation.

   (Wiley series on organizational assessment and change,
ISSN 0194-0210)
   "A Wiley-Interscience publication."
   Includes bibliographical and indexes.
   1. Quality of work life—Case studies. 2. Organizational change—Case studies. 3. Employees' representa-
tion in management—Case studies. 4. Machinery in
industry—Case studies. I. Nieva, Veronica F.
II. Lawler, Edward E. III. Title. IV. Series.

HD4905.P47 1983   658.1'1   82-17548
ISBN 0-471-05204-3

Printed in the United States of America

10 9 8 7 6 5 4 3 2 1

To the men and women of Centerton

Series Preface

THE ORGANIZATIONAL ASSESSMENT AND CHANGE SERIES is concerned with informing and furthering contemporary debate on the effectiveness of work organizations and the quality of life they provide for their members. Of particular relevance is the adaptation of work organizations to changing social aspirations and economic constraints. There has been a phenomenal growth of interest in the quality of work life and productivity in recent years. Issues that not long ago were the quiet concern of a few academics and a few leaders in unions and management have become issues of broad public interest. They have intruded upon broadcast media prime time, lead newspaper and magazine columns, the houses of Congress, and the board rooms of firms and unions alike.

A thorough discussion of what organizations should be like and how they can be improved must encompass many issues. Some are basic moral and ethical questions: What is the responsibility of an organization to its employees? What, after all, is a "good job"? How should it be decided that some might benefit from and others pay for gains in the quality of work life? Should there be a public policy on the matter? Yet others are concerned with the strategies and tactics of bringing about changes in organizational life, the advocates of alternative approaches being numerous, vocal, and controversial. Still others are concerned with the task of measurement and assessment on grounds that the choices to be made by leaders, the assessment of consequences, and the bargaining of equities must be informed by reliable, comprehensive, and relevant information of kinds not now readily available.

The Wiley Series on Organizational Assessment and Change is concerned with all aspects of the debate on how organizations should be managed, changed, and controlled. It includes books on organizational effectiveness and the study of organizational changes that represent new approaches to organization design and process. The volumes in the series have in common a concern with work organizations, a focus on change and the dynamics of change, an assumption that diverse social and personal interests need to be taken into account in discussions of organizational effectiveness, and a view that concrete cases and quantitative data are essential ingredients in a lucid debate. As such, these books consider a broad but integrated set of issues and ideas. They are intended to be read by managers, union officials, researchers, consultants, policy makers, students, and others seriously concerned with organizational assessment and change.

This volume, *Managing Creation: The Challenge of Building a New Organization*, provides a detailed and intimate account of the start-up of a new organization with the intention to incorporate many of the attributes associated with high quality of work life. Events are followed over a considerable span of time, during which the organization acquired a core staff, took on successive waves of new employees requiring training and indoctrination, got its technologies up and operating, and took on some stable properties best described as the unique culture of a maturing organization. The account includes several features not commonly included in such case studies. There is attention to the individuality of key people and the influence of personalities on the emerging organizational characteristics. The interplay between complex technological systems and the formation of their associated human systems is described. From the observations there is developed the beginning of a theory about the stages of organizational formation and the kinds of issues encountered at each stage. The theory and related observations are employed to help understand why the organizations conformed to some of the original aspirations and intentions of the founders but deviated in other respects. The book will be of interest to readers professionally concerned with the creation and changing of organizations as well as those interested in the observed variety of organizational systems and the forces that generate differences among them.

EDWARD E. LAWLER III
STANLEY E. SEASHORE

Beverly Hills, California
Ann Arbor, Michigan
January 1983

Preface

This book has two dominant and interwoven themes: organizational creation and participative management. Its origins can be traced to our efforts to understand the process of creation in a medical products laboratory that was dedicated—from its inception—to worker involvement through collaborative decision making.

This research, originally designed to evaluate the effectiveness of a Quality of Work Life program introduced by an independent consulting team, led us to questions much broader than those posed by the initial study. The events that transpired during our research on "Centerton"—the name we have given to the organization—stimulated our thinking about a number of other questions. Were the tumultuous early days of Centerton characteristic of the process of creation in other new organizations? Were there existing theories that would have enabled us to predict the evolution of the fledgling organization? How did Centerton's technology interact with its attempt to use participative management in the start-up process? And, finally, what are the implications of the Centerton experience for other organizations with one or more of its distinctive characteristics: advanced technology, high involvement, and infancy?

In pursuing these questions we encountered a disparate set of experiences and theoretical perspectives. In the process, we learned a good deal about the issues we had raised, and perhaps as much about our own reactions to the complex task of theory construction and research. It is our hope that the results of these experiences will be useful to practitioners, academicians, and others who are concerned with the topics we have struggled to understand.

The book speaks directly to the theme of organizational creation. It proposes a framework for conceptualizing the process, and derives a set of action implications designed to address the predictable growing pains of new settings. It also identifies conditions for the effective use of high involvement organization designs, taking account of considerations such as the nature of the organization's technology and its current life cycle stage. Finally, the book deals with many of the specific questions that arise in evaluating the effects of behavioral science programs, and with the larger issue of the societal significance of the Quality of Work Life movement.

In all, it has been an ambitious undertaking. We are glad to have embarked on the adventure and both elated and saddened that it is over. If our ideas genuinely stimulate others—whether to agree or disagree—then there will be more joy that the work is done and less sorrow that the journey has ended.

DENNIS N. T. PERKINS
VERONICA F. NIEVA
EDWARD E. LAWLER III

New Haven, Connecticut
Rockville, Maryland
Los Angeles, California
January 1983

Acknowledgments

The number of individuals who have contributed to our enterprise seems extraordinarily large. At the Institute for Social Research, Cortland Cammann, Mark Fichman, John Klesh, and Gerry Ledford made a number of helpful comments on our initial assessment of the Centerton Quality of Work Life program. Gary Herline assisted in data collection and management; Doug Jenkins and Frank Andrews helped us wrestle with methodological problems; and Sherry Nelson did a superb job of coordinating the administrative parts of the project.

As our thinking about new organizations evolved, we were guided by the perspectives of others who have reflected on the topic of new settings. Seymour Sarason's seminal work, and his continuing role as an intellectual and spiritual *sensei*, were invaluable. Cary Cherniss, Rick Price, and John Hartman nurtured our early efforts and influenced our thinking. Clay Alderfer's and David Berg's research on underbounded systems contributed to our understanding of new organizations. Richard Hackman once called our theory of creation elegant, and his words were timely and inspirational. Phil Mirvis has—from beginning to end—done yeoman's work as consultant, gadfly, critic, jester, and muse.

We are also indebted to Anne Killoy and Linda Botte for indefatigable spirit in typing the manuscript; to Angela Parent for finding errors that are typically overlooked; and to Mary Daniello for her patience and skill in orchestrating the production process. Virginia Withey, by virtue of her editorial assistance and personal encouragement, became the *deus ex machina* of the book; indeed, she is *sui generis*. Holly Frances Perkins helped by continuing her tradition of both seeing and observing. Thanks, Poppet.

Finally, we acknowledge Robert Foster for his support as Department of Labor project officer; the consultants who established the Centerton Quality of Work Life program; and the Centerton employees who generously shared their time and insights so that the story might be told.

D. N. T. P.
V. F. N.
E. E. L. III

Contents

PART ONE

ORGANIZATIONAL CREATION AND WORKER INVOLVEMENT

Chapter One

Introduction

An important change has taken place in the way organizations are designed and managed in the United States. During the 1970s, a number of major American corporations established one or more new plants in a manner representing a radical break with tradition. From the start, these plants have stressed employee involvement, job enrichment, and participative management. The list of companies opening these new "Quality of Work Life"—or "high involvement"—plants reads like the *Fortune* 500. They include General Foods, Procter & Gamble, TRW, Dana Corporation, Rockwell, General Motors, Meads, and Cummins Engine. Although no one knows just how many organizations have created these innovative work settings, a good guess would be that at least 20 large corporations have started one or more, and that 100 or more are presently in existence.

The importance of these new plants may far outweigh their number. Some experts have suggested that they are the prototypes of organizations of the future; that they represent the American answer to the productivity and management challenges presented by such formidable international competitors as the Japanese and the Germans. However, not everyone agrees that these Quality of Work Life organizations represent a new wave in management; in fact, a few of the more visible Quality of Work Life plants (e.g., the Topeka General Foods plant) have been the focus of extensive controversy. Critics have questioned their economic effectiveness, the degree to which their organizational principles can be applied to other plants, and the extent to which they actually provide a high quality of work life.

These are all important issues, but they are not the only unanswered questions concerning new plants. New organizations also present an interesting research challenge. Until recently, there has been a paucity of research and theory about the creation of new organizations. Several seminal pieces have appeared in the last few years, but we still know relatively little about the nature of emergent organizations. Do they, for example, undergo predictable stages of growth? Is it possible to find strategies for improving the likelihood that new organizations will succeed or, at least, are there strategies for easing their growing pains? In particular, what is the potential of worker participation in facilitating the creation of new organizations?

This book deals with questions such as these: It is concerned both with the developmental characteristics of new organizations and the strengths and limitations of high involvement working environments. We begin by presenting, in Chapter 2, a conceptual framework for the evolution of new organizations. This theoretical discussion is followed by an intensive case description of a new plant—known as "Centerton"—that attempted to use high involvement as a means of achieving both greater productivity and a high quality of work life. We then present our assessment of the implementation of this program and its effects on the Centerton start-up process. In the final chapters, we summarize our views on the creation of high involvement organizations and strategies for behavioral science intervention in new work settings.

Before turning to this theoretical and empirical material, however, we will provide a brief background sketch of the new, high involvement plant. This background material was derived from visits to 10 other high involvement plants, from interviews with individuals associated with some 20 additional organizations, and from published descriptions of several other organizations (see Davis & Sullivan, 1980; Poza & Markus, 1980). From these sources we were able to develop a "composite sketch" of this new organizational form. The characteristics which follow do not fit every organization perfectly, but they do enable one to appreciate the character of a typical high involvement organization.

CHARACTERISTICS OF HIGH INVOLVEMENT PLANTS

One of the most interesting things about the new Quality of Work Life plants we studied is the common approach taken with regard to certain design issues. There seems to be a consensus among most organizations about a number of basic practices, since there are a number of innovations common to all—or almost all—of the new Quality of Work Life plants. Our review of these features will illustrate the way in which specific areas of management have been affected, as well as how these plants differ from their more traditional counterparts.

Employee Selection

The traditional selection approach has, for the most part, been abandoned in the typical high involvement organization. Instead of having the Personnel Department screen, test, and select applicants, the company uses a process designed to help job applicants make valid decisions about whether they would "fit" into potential positions. In addition, rank and file employees are directly involved in making selection decisions.

This nontraditional selection process emphasizes acquainting job candidates with the details of the jobs they may fill and the nature of the managerial style that will be used in the plant, so that they can decide realistically whether a particular position is right for them. In most plants, a group interview is held by the managers and the candidate's potential co-workers. Once the plant becomes operational, this same approach to selection continues, and work team members assume responsibility for the selection of new members of their teams.

Egalitarian Perquisites

There is frequently a strong egalitarian emphasis in the way work and leisure areas of the new plants are designed. For example, rather than providing separate areas for managers to eat and spend their nonwork hours, a conscious effort is made to see that everyone uses the same dining, rest room, and recreational facilities. In many organizations, this is combined with entrances and parking areas that are used by all employees. Special parking spaces, dining rooms, and rest rooms are conspicuous by their absence. By avoiding these obvious signs of rank, a clear message is communicated that—at least in terms of the physical plant and perquisites—a relatively egalitarian system exists.

The Physical Arrangement of Work

In some of the organizations we studied, considerable thought had been given to plant layout to ensure that it was compatible with the social system being created. This emphasis was perhaps not as common as the others we have mentioned, but a concern for spatial arrangements was an important characteristic in a number—about a third—of the plants we surveyed. In its most complete manifestation, equipment, walls, lounges—indeed, the total organization—were structured according to sociotechnical design concepts. Most designs ensured that groups could form naturally around the production process, with clearly defined inputs and outputs.

The Volvo plant in Kalmar, Sweden is perhaps the best known example of a plant designed according to these principles. According to this design concept, groups complete entire parts of the automobile production process in their own work areas. These spaces typically include team meeting rooms, offices for the foremen, and separate entrances and locker room facilities.

In some of the plants we observed, an effort was made to hire some members of the work force early enough so that they could participate in decisions about the layout of machinery, equipment, and the recreational and personal areas of the plant. The idea was to capture employee suggestions from the start, and to use collaborative decision making to improve the design of the plant. In some cases, this was accomplished by asking employees from already existing plants to participate in the design of the new ones.

Personnel Policies

Most new plants place a high value on employment stability. Consequently, they make an initial commitment to all regular employees. This agreement, based on the assumption that layoffs have detrimental effects on productivity and job satisfaction, typically stipulates that every effort will be made to see that—with the exception of performance or disciplinary problems—no one will be terminated involuntarily. Because of economic realities, the organization usually stops short of assuring people that they will never be laid off. But the expectation is created that layoffs will occur only as a last resort.

This policy has been implemented in a number of ways. For example, temporary employees can be used in times of high business volume. During slow periods, regular employees can be given maintenance or even make-work jobs. In some cases in which a force reduction has seemed inevitable, employees have elected to shut down the plant for a limited period to avoid terminating a few individuals. However the policy is implemented, the underlying premise is usually stated as follows: "If we want employees to make a commitment to the organization, we have to make a commitment to them."

Job Design

In all of the plants we examined, a substantial effort was made to see that individuals were given challenging, motivating, and satisfying jobs. In a few cases, this was accomplished through individually based job enrichment approaches emphasizing personal responsibility in producing a complete, meaningful piece of work. In most cases, however, job enrichment involved the creation of autonomous work groups.

With this approach, teams rather than individuals are given responsibility for manufacturing a whole product. Teams are self-managing in the sense that they decide who will perform tasks on a given day; they set their own production goals and are often responsible for controlling quality, purchasing, and absenteeism. In most cases there is a strong emphasis on job rotation, and it is expected that most individuals on the team will learn to do all the jobs that fall in that team's work areas.

In some plants an effort is made to add interesting tasks to work that would otherwise be monotonous. In one plant, for example, maintenance jobs were made part of the same job family as warehousing. This change ensured that no one was required to spend all of his or her time doing the relatively boring and routine maintenance tasks. The expected result of the team approach is that individuals will feel responsible for a significant part of the organizational work, experience a sense of self-control, and receive feedback about how effectively the team operates as a unit.

Pay Systems

Most plants have taken an unusual approach in establishing base pay levels for employees. Instead of a traditional job evaluation system, in which jobs are scored according to their characteristics for the purpose of determining a common pay rate for equivalent jobs in the plant, the skills of each individual are assessed independently. Everyone begins at the same salary, and receives greater compensation as he or she learns new skills. When this system is combined with job rotation, a person doing a relatively low level job may be quite highly paid because he or she is capable of performing a large number of other, more skilled tasks.

This approach has two main advantages. First, it tends to create a flexible, highly trained work force that can adapt to most changes in product demand and staffing since replacements are readily available. In addition, it contributes to the development of the work team by giving employees broader knowledge of the plant operation. This is important because it enables individuals to participate in a greater number of decisions and fosters identification with the goals of the plant.

In about half of the new plants we examined, judgments regarding whether or not an individual had mastered a new job well enough to deserve a salary increase were left to the members of his or her own team. This approach to pay decisions reinforces the participative management style that is critical to the operation of high involvement plants.

A few of these plants have taken additional steps to tie pay to performance. Some have introduced a merit component into their skill based pay systems. Several others have introduced plant wide profit sharing plans after having achieved stable performance history. Organization wide sharing of productivity gains is congruent with the team concept of management as well as the general participative principles that underlie the design of these organizations. Thus we would expect that, as new plants mature and establish stable base periods for measuring productivity gains, the use of these gain sharing plans will become more common.

Organizational Structure

A striking feature of these plants is their structural hierarchy. All the organizations we studied have located the Plant Manager only a few levels above the production workers. In some cases, the role of foreman has been eliminated completely. In others, foremen report directly to the Plant Manager, and such traditional intermediate levels as General Foreman and Superintendent have been eliminated.

Where there are no foremen, several teams usually report to a single supervisor and the teams are considered self-managed. In most cases, an elected team leader is responsible for communicating with the rest of the organization. This person undertakes the time-consuming task of lateral integration with other functional and line departments; this role would typically be an important responsibility for a first-line supervisor (see Walton & Schlesinger, 1979).

In contrast to the functional organization structure of many traditional organizations, high involvement plants tend to be organized around a product or geographic location. The intent of this design approach is to give individuals the responsibility for "something"—rather than for a less tangible function, such as maintenance or engineering. This system is expected to provide more meaningful job structures, and to encourage deeper commitment to the work.

Because of the way they are structured, most high involvement plants have a relatively small number of indirect labor employees. For example, since some scheduling is done by the teams, fewer people are needed for centralized scheduling. Since many of such staff functions are handled by the work teams rather than by specialists, requirements for supporting staff can be significantly decreased. This reduction is, of course, somewhat offset by increased requirements for direct labor.

Approach to Training

All the new Quality of Work Life plants place a heavy emphasis upon training, career planning, and the personal growth and development of employees. This is usually supported with extensive on-site training programs and strong encouragement for individuals to take off-the-job training. This off-site training is often financially supported by the organization.

Some interesting concepts in employee education have developed in these high involvement organizations. In some, individuals are trained in the economics of the industry and, when they complete relevant courses, are rewarded with higher pay. Interpersonal skills training and team development opportunities are also frequently offered, since both are consistent with the goal of producing individuals who are able to work in a collaborative, high involvement organization.

Regular career planning sessions are also scheduled. In some plants, this may involve an employee's presenting a personal career development plan to his or her team members; in others, the process is handled by a manager. This strong emphasis on individual development often engenders the feeling that personal growth is an important and legitimate part of organizational life; sometimes this spirit is so pervasive that it extends to both job related and non-job related skills.

Open Information System

Most organizations collect a great deal of information about their financial performance. In many traditional organizations, this information is seen only by a select group of senior managers. This is not the case in most new high involvement plants. In these settings, information is widely shared and often used for goal setting. This approach, when combined with economic education, creates a working environment in which employees can truly understand how well the plant is doing. Thus they can experience the satisfaction of being part of a larger team and can relate their efforts to the performance of the total plant.

Plant Wide Participative Council

In any organization, problems inevitably arise that cannot be resolved by individual work groups. In many new plants, these issues are dealt with by a plant wide group of employee representatives. The members of this group are elected by work teams and are asked to act as communication links to the primary work groups. This council can also serve as a sounding board for new ideas and as a place for the team to raise issues that are of potential concern to employees throughout the plant—for example, personnel policies, pay system changes, and the financial performance of the organization.

Management Philosophy

Most of the characteristics we have mentioned so far are simply operational elements needed to implement a more general philosophy of participative management. In practice, this is realized when decisions are pushed as far down in the organization as possible. As we have indicated, in the new, high involvement plants, this means that purchasing decisions are made or influenced by line workers, and that even personnel selection decisions are made participatively. There are some cases, however, in which decision making cannot be done effectively at lower levels in the organization; in these instances, issues are discussed by all employees and every view is seriously considered before a final decision is reached. For example, a number of plants have delayed establishing certain personnel policies until the work force is hired and everyone can participate in developing them.

Although there is considerable variation in specific practices, the operational form of this decision making structure represents a more fundamental commitment to a set of beliefs about the nature of good management. This philosophy emphasizes the worth of each individual and places considerable faith in the potential contribution of ideas generated by rank and file workers. This style of participative management is more than a collection of techniques for decision making: It is, rather, a philosophy of management that envisions collaborative "spirit" as the cornerstone of organizational effectiveness and individual growth.

SUMMARY AND CONCLUSIONS

The new Quality of Work Life plants differ from traditional plants in a number of important ways. Table 1-1, which summarizes some of the design features typically found in these organizations, provides an indication of the range of organizational variables that have been affected.

This list makes it clear that a broad spectrum of basic organizational building blocks have been affected. The reward system, the structure, the physical layout, the personnel management system, and the nature of jobs are all different in important ways. Because so many aspects of these organizations have been altered, it is not an exaggeration to say that, when combined, they lead to a fundamentally different kind of organization.

It is important to stress, however, that the new Quality of Work Life plant is still regarded by many as an experimental concept. These organizations are continually being modified by experience and changes in local conditions. Thus, although

Table 1-1   Characteristics of a High Involvement Work Setting

Organizational structure
  Flat
  Lean
  Mini-enterprise oriented
  Team based
  Participative council or structure
Job design
  Individually enriched or
  Self-managing teams
Information system
  Open
  Inclusive
  Tied to jobs
  Decentralized
  Participatively set goals and standards
Career system
  Tracks and counseling available
  Open job posting
Selection
  Realistic job preview
  Team based
  Potential and process skill oriented
Training
  Heavy commitment
  Peer training
  Economic education
  Interpersonal skills
Reward system
  Open
  Skill based
  Gain sharing or ownership
  Flexible benefits
  All salary
  Egalitarian perquisites
Personnel policies
  Stability of employment
  Participatively established through
    representative group
Physical layout
  Egalitarian
  Safe and pleasant
  Congruent with organizational structure

an identifiable set of innovations is being tested, it is clear that each organization has adapted these concepts in ways that render its management system and overall design unique. The "new wave" of plants is not, therefore, a monolithic movement: It is more a small sea of breakers, from which will evolve an organizational form suited to the demands of its human and economic environments.

Centerton, the medical products laboratory whose history we documented, represents one such setting; its history will be described shortly. Before turning to the Centerton story, however, we will move from our discussion of high involvement organizations to the subject of organizational creation, the second major theme of this book. Chapter 2 develops a framework for viewing a new organization as one of a class of emergent social systems. Then, in Chapter 3, both themes of participation and creation converge in our recounting of the Centerton experience.

Chapter Two

New Organizations: A Conceptual Framework

The creation of new organizations is a topic of considerable interest to social scientists (Heller & Monahan, 1977; Rappaport, 1977), but relatively little has been written about the nature of emergent social settings. Although those who have created new organizations have extensive firsthand knowledge, little of their expertise has found its way into the literature of social science. As Sarason (1972) notes:

> One of the thorny obstacles to understanding . . . the creation of settings is the lack of well-described instances. If one were to use the literary utopias as examples of description telling us how and why things were done, one would have to conclude that the number of adequate descriptions . . . is almost nonexistent. (p. 21)

If the supply of case descriptions is limited, then the state of theoretical development is equally inchoate. The recent work of Kimberly, Miles, and associates (1980) represents an important step forward in the effort to chart the course of the organizational life cycle. But we are still far away from a general theory of organizational growth (Kimberly et al., 1980).

This paper proposes a schema of organizational growth intended to integrate the developmental events and issues that appear to be typical of emergent social systems. It begins by describing a set of common themes that characterize social systems of varying size, and it concludes with a general framework for viewing the development of new settings. Later, in Chapter 10, this model is used as a basis for outlining a set of practical implications for the architects of new organizations.

The model is based on three classes of developmental theories: First, research on the emergence of new organizational forms; second, the literature on the evolution of small groups; and, finally, conceptions of individual growth.

Of the three classes of theories considered, organizational perspectives are the most obviously relevant. But it appears that social systems of varying size share a set of common developmental attributes. Sarason (1972), for example, argues:

> The characteristics of the . . . group that I have presented are highly similar to those of any new setting. In describing other instances of the creation of settings the language and emphasis would be different . . . but the characteristics would be surprisingly similar. For example, the fear of being in danger from outside forces, the sense of being or wanting to be different and better or even unique, the desire to grow and amass people or things, to be primarily future oriented—these are some of the characteristics to be found in any instance of the creation of settings. Entering into marriage or starting a new university or new business is obviously different from organizing a setting for the purpose of overthrowing a society . . ., and yet they share certain common characteristics or problems. Amoebas are obviously different from elephants, and both are different from man, but all do share certain common properties. (p. 9, footnote)

This view is shared by other behavioral scientists. Alderfer (1976), for example, observes that persons, groups, and organizations may be conceptualized as open systems, and Miller's (1965, 1978) work on the properties of living systems points toward a similar conclusion. If regularities extend from dyadic exchanges to social revolution, then it is a reasonable undertaking to examine the possibility of common ontogenetic characteristics: It would not be surprising to find similar patterns of development across several levels of analysis.

STAGES IN THE GROWTH OF EMERGENT SOCIAL SYSTEMS

The model to be described proposes that social systems progress through a series of five developmental stages. This movement is not inexorable, and a number of moderating variables—to be discussed later—may affect the course and speed of development. Nevertheless, we believe that the typical social setting is likely to experience predictable periods of evolution, and that a set of developmental issues associated with each phase will become salient during the early life of the setting. Each of these phases will be described in the following paragraphs, along with examples drawn from the literature on organizational, group, and individual development.

These examples, to be sure, do not represent a single, unified perspective. Within each level of analysis can be found a spate of competing, conflicting, and sometimes complementary theories. In examining the small group literature, for example, Hill and Gruner (1973) found over 100 articles that offered a clear theoretical statement on the nature of group development. Although organizational theorists have been less prolific, models of individual development abound, and it is safe to say that no universal, all purpose model has emerged.

Our purpose, however, is not to review the extensive literature in each field. Rather, it is to suggest a framework derived from major theoretical works that we found to be both influential and amenable to comparative analysis. The appropriateness of our choices can be determined by the validity of the resulting model, as tested by its relevance to the developmental events observed at Centerton and its utility as a tool for understanding the creation of other organizations.

The First Stage of Development: Utopian Fantasy

Theorists such as Greiner (1972) and Sarason (1972) describe an initial period of organizational life characterized by creativity, missionary zeal, and frequently, unrealistic expectations about the future. Greiner (1972) describes this stage as one in which communication is frequent and informal, participants work long hours, and financial rewards are modest. It is during this frenetic initial period that the core group is formed and relationships between leaders and their "families" are negotiated. It is also during this period that seeds of future problems are sown. In particular, the stage for later developmental crises is set by unexamined assumptions of the recruitment process, failure to establish adequate mechanisms for governance, and the "myth of unlimited resources" (Sarason, 1972, p. 91).

The conception of an initial fantasy stage is echoed in the literature of small groups. Based on their observation of interpersonal behavior in groups from an academic setting, Hartman and Gibbard (1974b) identify five stages of development. The first developmental period, that of "mystical fusion," is seen from the authors' psychodynamic perspective as a desire to establish a sense of "magical fullness" that is characteristic of the early mother–child symbiosis. "It is the return to Paradise, the achievement of Nirvana" (p. 319).

This initial fantasy of mystical fusion gives way to a stage characterized by the attribution of omnipotence to the group leader. In this second period of "deification," the leader is singled out as an object of dependency; this is a perceptual shift that distinguishes the phase from its preceding period of undifferentiated fusion.

Drawing on Bion's (1959) earlier work, Bennis and Shepard (1974) describe a similar period in group life and posit an initial subphase characterized by "dependence–flight" behavior. During this first stage, group members seek security and reassurance from the leader and do not challenge his or her wisdom, power, or competence. Although this time is filled with hidden anxiety, it is characterized by hope—hope that the leader holds a grand plan that contains the "rules of the game" and the mission of the group. Group members turn to the leader, therefore, to resolve the ambiguity and discomfort that pervade this first developmental period.

It is interesting to note that Bennis and Shepard's (1974) conception of small group development and the Hartman and Gibbard (1974a) schema both reveal similarities with theories of the individual. Bennis and Shepard draw on the Sullivanian definition of personal maturity, arguing that a mature group—like a mature individual—is able to analyze interpersonal experience and achieve security and satisfaction without undue threat to self-esteem. Hartman and Gibbard (1974a) use a somewhat different theoretical point of departure, but propose a similar sequence of events. Their conceptualization is grounded in the theory of object relations, specifically the progressive differentiation of self and object representations. Again, the relationship with individual growth is emphasized:

> The analogy between this scheme of group development and early ego development is imperfect but provocative. Just as the object relations of the developing child move from an undifferentiated state in which self and object representations are fused, to a state of part-objects and partial fusion of self and others, to relatively permanent differentiation of self and object representations, groups evidence analogous processes. (p. 175)

It may seem inappropriate to compare individual development with the growth of larger social systems, since a considerable portion of individual maturation is genetically programmed in a way that group and organizational growth is not. But theories of the individual deal with emergent "social systems" in a very real sense. The development of the child is embedded in a complex set of social interactions that involve parents, peers, siblings, teachers, and other significant figures. The social context has a direct, and in some cases, overwhelming impact on the course of personal growth. Thus it is reasonable to think of individual development as a special case in the comparative analysis of social structures.

This psychosocial schedule is clearly seen in the work of Erik Erikson. The Eriksonian (1963) framework posits a series of critical steps, or turning points, that are considered to be characteristic of the human life cycle. Each element of "psychosocial strength" is assumed to exist from the beginning of life, but rises to ascendance and resolution during its appropriate developmental period. Each virtue can be understood only in the context of other stages, and the evolutionary sequence is fixed. There is, nevertheless, some "room for variation in tempo and intensity . . . . Each such acceleration or (relative) retardation, however, is assumed to have a modifying influence on all later stages" (Erikson, 1963, p. 272). Thus an individual may be precocious and experience a point of decision before the predicted life moment; conversely, choice points may be retarded, and one may regress toward an earlier life theme.

The initial Eriksonian period, "trust versus mistrust," is a crucial time of confidence and naiveté. As was true of the group and organizational theories cited, this initial period is characterized by faith in the future, and especially, by hope. Thus

> a reasonably coherent world provides the faith which is transmitted to the infants in a way conducive to the initial strength of hope, that is, the enduring predisposition to believe in the attainability of primal wishes in spite of the anarchic urges and rages of dependency. The shortest formulation of the identity gain of earliest childhood may well be: I am what hope I have and give. (Erikson, 1968, pp. 106–107)

This initial stage of individual development shares the basic character of small group and organizational schemas. In fact, Erikson further argues that each successive stage of individual development is conceptually related to the institutional structure of society, and that this similarity is not accidental. He contends that the association exists precisely because the human life cycle and human institutions have evolved together in a mutually supportive, symbiotic form (Erikson, 1968).

It is not difficult to find well-documented instances of this initial fantasy period in organizational life. The National Institute of Education, for example, was created with the expectation that it would significantly alter the character of American education. As Sproull, Weiner, and Wolf (1978) observe,

> The process of creation . . . endows a new agency with a sense of significance. For the people who come to staff it, its creation takes on an air of heroic and historic inevitability. The fact of its existence is proof that powerful people believe in its importance. (p. 71)

This belief structure is further buttressed by the rhetoric of creation. They describe the Commissioner of the Office of Education as "almost poetic in his enthusiasm: We will have in NIE a fountain of new and useful knowledge" (p. 64).

An equally romantic theme is reflected in Goldenberg's (1971) account of the Residential Youth Center, an experimental project run in association with Yale's Psycho-Educational Clinic. He writes:

> For most of the Center's original staff, the RYC was indeed a "love affair," an undertaking which, for all its moments of panic and uncertainty, possessed the binding qualities of a revolution. We were (or at least felt ourselves to be) a little band of rebels, scornful of tradition and duly unimpressed by the accomplishments of those who had preceded us—a group of missionaries committed to the creation of a very personal and earthbound utopia. (p. 42)

Goldenberg's words convey the passion with which the creators of new organizations approach their task. Whether the dreams of creation will be realized is, of course, another question. There is reason to believe that utopian expectations are not likely to be met. But the emotions associated with this period undoubtedly serve an important purpose, and it may be that—without such utopian beliefs—few people would have the temerity to create new settings.

The Second Stage of Development: Challenge to Authority

This hopeful, initial period is likely to end with the emergence of turbulence and conflict. Greiner (1972) contends that the first period of creativity will be truncated by the onset of an organizational revolution, an event precipitated by: increasing organizational size; a decrease in informal communication; loss of dedication on the part of those who have shared the dream of creation; and the unsuitable "temperament" of those who initially founded the organization. Failure to accomplish unrealistic goals, coupled with difficulty in operationalizing the philosophy of the organization, will eventually lead to a breakdown in managerial control. If the organization is to survive, it must be rescued from the ambiguity and confusion of this "crisis of leadership."

Sarason's (1972) work also supports the thesis that a leadership crisis is to a large extent inevitable. He contends that two problems are commonly cited as reasons for the breakdown: (1) internal mismanagement and broken promises; and (2) the work of subversive external forces. Sarason argues, however, that the etiology of "organizational craziness" lies elsewhere. Rather, he suggests it is the failure to confront predictable problems of the utopian period that contributes to later trauma. Thus the fundamental problem is the failure to establish mechanisms—such as a governance structure and sensing systems—capable of accommodating the organizational turbulence that predictably occurs early in the organizational life cycle.

This period of conflict is also anticipated in the small group literature. Bennis and Shepard (1974) theorized that the initial stage of dependency is followed by the emergence of "counterdependency–flight." This is a period in which group members are preoccupied with the issue of power. The theory predicts the emergence of two major subgroups that will be unable to agree on the issues of structure and leadership. The polarization ends when the leader is challenged and, at least temporarily, rejected by both dependent and counterdependent group members. To explain the outcome of this symbolic rebellion, Bennis and Shepard draw on Freud's myth of the primal horde: The group member who foments the revolt becomes the triumphant hero, and a sense of solidarity and involvement pervades the group.

The occurrence of such a rebellion is foreseen in Hartman and Gibbard's (1974a) schema, and given empirical support by their (1974b) process analysis scoring system. Their theoretical explanation for the leader–member conflict is again based on object relations theory: "All that is bad, frustrating, malevolent is put into the leader, and he is symbolically destroyed" (p. 39).

A crisis of power appears as well in the second stage of Erikson's schema of human development. In this developmental period, the dependent child experiences the will to selfhood, namely, the need to stand on his own feet and test his strength against that of his parents. In this battle for autonomy, "sinister forces are leashed and unleashed, especially in the guerrilla warfare of unequal wills, for the child is often unequal to his own violent will and parent and child are often unequal to one another" (Erikson, 1968, p. 107). Thus the conflictual period predicted by organizational and small group theorists has its analogue in the ontogeny of individual development.

The Third Stage of Development: Resolution

In a successful social system, the turbulent period of crisis and rebellion will give way to a period of stability and growth. Greiner (1972) refers to this stage as "growth through direction." It is during this period that job assignments and organizational structure are better defined, standardized control and incentive systems are introduced, and communication is formalized as hierarchical structures are established. At this stage in the organizational life cycle, imperfections in the system are accepted or at least tolerated for a time.

The ascendance of a period of tranquility is once again predicted by research on the development of small groups. Bennis and Shepard's (1974) period of "resolution–catharsis" marks the end of a preoccupation with dependency and power. In the beginning of this period, the atmosphere is relaxed and peaceful. Tension is assiduously avoided in the service of solidarity, and the primary task is one of recovery from the stresses of the second stage.

This period of mutual harmony and acceptance is, in reality, a myth. Interpersonal conflict has been temporarily masked by the struggle for leadership, and a new polarity will develop. This second struggle pits the "overpersonals"—those who are prepared to sacrifice their individual identities—against the "counterpersonals," who resist the sacrifice. During this third stage of consolidation, however, direct confrontation is postponed.

Hartman and Gibbard (1974a) characterize this period of resolution with a maternal theme. From their perspective, group members strive to replace conflict with a state of nurturance and security. Negative aspects of the group, such as hostility and the fear of being overwhelmed, are defended against, and positive elements are emphasized. During this stage, a "group as mother" provides the warmth and protectiveness needed to heal the wounds inflicted during the preceding conflictual period.

Their conception of calm following the storm of conflict is generally consistent with the Eriksonian schema. Erikson predicts that the child's crisis of autonomy will be followed by a period of "initiative," characterized as a

> new miracle of vigorous unfolding, which constitutes a new hope and a new responsibility . . . a crisis, more or less beset with fumbling and fear, is resolved, in that the child suddenly seems to "grow together" both in his person and in his body. (Erikson, 1963, p. 255)

In this stage of growth, the previously defiant child is able to move ahead, to plan and execute tasks with a coherent sense of purpose.

The stability found during this stage of life continues into latency when the school age child develops social skills. During the latency period, a sense of industry is established, and the experience of successful interpersonal negotiation results in a new psychosocial strength: "competence." In this phase of development, violent biological drives are dormant, "But it is only a lull before the storm of puberty, when all the earlier drives reemerge in a new combination" (Erikson, 1963, p. 260).

The Fourth Stage of Growth: Intergroup Conflict

Greiner's (1972) idea of "growth through direction," the third period in our developmental model, ultimately ends in a second crisis. This new disturbance originates in needs for autonomy: Members of the organization find themselves thwarted by cumbersome procedures and a centralized hierarchy. These constraints lead to dissatisfaction, disenchantment, and in some cases, departure from the organization.

Sarason's (1972) analysis of organizational growing pains further illuminates the sources of this second crisis. One problem can be traced to ambiguities in the contract between the leader and members of the core group. This lack of clarity increases the risk of intergroup conflict, since each group member is likely to develop exaggerated expectations about his or her future role in the organization. This confusion is compounded by the needs of various subgroups to rally around their leaders in an attempt to solidify their identities. This activity sets the stage for a parochial orientation that will eventually obscure the needs of the organization as a whole. These intergroup tensions will ultimately surface as conflicts regarding the issues of resource allocation, influence with the leader, and explicit goals and values.

Goldenberg's (1971) account of the Residential Youth Center underscores the way in which inconsistencies in resource allocation and governance can exacerbate intergroup conflict. The operation of the Residential Youth Center was based on "horizontality," an egalitarian principle in which responsibilities are equally shared. All staff members carried equal case loads, shared administrative duties, "lived in," ran evening programs, and so forth.

The salary structure was, however, inconsistent. The paraprofessionals received significantly less pay than the professionals doing equivalent work. Predictably, this increased intergroup tensions:

> The discrepancy between the RYC's formal structure and its underlying assumptions facilitated the development of what might be called "compensatory pecking-order behavior"; that is, behavior in which certain staff members, "robbed" of the equality which would have been theirs had the setting been structurally organized in a way that was consistent with its internal processes, sought to erect an "informal" status hierarchy barrier between themselves and the rest of the staff. Thus, for example, RYC workers began to relate to live-in counselors as if they

(the live-ins) were less important to the setting. The live-ins, on the other hand, began to view themselves as increasingly left out of the Center's decisionmaking process and became resentful of the "high-hattedness" of the RYC workers. It was, in short, a situation in which people who were actually working in very similar ways felt compelled to justify (and reinforce) whatever differences they could find between them. (Goldenberg, 1971, p. 433)

Of course, these conditions could produce intergroup conflict in a mature organization as well. But the effects of these frictions seem to be particularly great in new settings.

The specter of intergroup conflict is also found in the Bennis and Shepard (1974) formulation of group development. By the end of the "enchantment" period, two subgroups have emerged. Beneath the polarization, both the "overpersonals" and "counterpersonals" share a common anxiety about the dangers of intimacy. This fear manifests itself in disparaging remarks about the group or its raison d'etre, poor group morale, boredom, and absenteeism. Bennis and Shepard argue that these behaviors are only symptoms of a defense against the anxiety associated with intimate interpersonal relations.

This theme is echoed by Hartman and Gibbard (1974a), whose "utopian" period is followed by a time of intense group rivalry and concern about the dangers of group intimacy. However, the dynamics of this "bisexual" stage are said to emanate from a "pairing fantasy" that fuses dependent and sexual needs in an effort to avoid reliance on other group members.

Many of the themes previously described are reflected in later stages of the Eriksonian schema. Issues of individual identity vis-à-vis the group, intimacy, sexuality, and intergroup conflict become salient with the onset of puberty and the beginning of youth. It is here, during the conflictual period between childhood and adulthood, that the issue of identity emerges with singular intensity. This period is rife with intergroup conflict, as adolescents struggle with the concept of fidelity. It is also a time of falling in love, and of cruelty toward "all those who are 'different' in skin color or cultural background, in taste and gifts, and often in such petty aspects of dress and gesture as have been temporarily selected as *the* signs of an in-grouper" (Erikson, 1963, p. 262). At this point, the child is able to rely on the group for support in his or her ongoing task of separation from parents. Thus the intensity of this period reflects a broad struggle for identity which includes differentiation from parents, discrimination among peers, and individuation within a chosen referent group.

Successful negotiation of this conflictual period prepares the adolescent for young adulthood and for the sacrifices and responsibilities necessary for commitment to significant relationships. In this period of growth the issue of intimacy is confronted directly. The resolution of previous conflicts should have prepared the secure individual to deal with fears of ego loss in times of self-abandon—such as those occurring in intimate friendships and sexual fusion (Erikson, 1963). Now he or she must choose between love and isolation, affiliation and distance. Those who overcome this developmental challenge are free to progress into maturity and old age, and to face the attendant concerns of generativity and integrity.

The fourth stage of development may be characterized, then, as a period of intergroup conflict following a phase of relatively undisturbed growth. Explanations for this second point of discontinuity vary across levels of analysis—organization, group, and individual—and among theorists. The broad picture that emerges, however, is a consistent pattern of interpersonal and intergroup upheaval.

The Final Stage of Development: Quasi-Stationary Equilibrium

At what point does a new organization become "mature," that is, outgrow those special qualities that are characteristic of a new setting? The answer is not entirely clear, and a similar ambiguity is reflected in debates about establishing legal drinking and voting ages.

Theories of individual growth have the advantage of biological anchors to describe the chronology of development. For Erikson, adulthood begins with his seventh stage, the polarity of "generativity versus stagnation." Adulthood continues into old age, where the psychosocial strength of "wisdom" is derived from the opposing forces of "integrity" and "despair."

The small group theories cited in this chapter also describe the life cycle of a time-limited social system. Bennis and Shepard's (1974) final stage of "consensual validation" was derived from observation of the approaching conclusion of a training course that dictated a method of self-evaluation. Successful completion of this activity depended on the resolution of conflicts regarding authority and intimacy; if these issues were successfully negotiated, the ultimate goal of valid interpersonal communication could be realized.

Hartman and Gibbard's (1974a) final phase of "messianism" is similarly based on the dynamics of a time-limited group. They believe that the theme of this final period is grounded in a desire to ward off impending disintegration; thus the group creates the fantasy of a messiah who will bring a new sense of hope and purpose.

The organizational literature is not, of course, based on limited life cycles that can be predicted with reliability. Greiner (1972) does posit later stages of growth—the last ending in a crisis of "?"—but he describes this final phase only in general terms. It is thought to center on the "psychological saturation" of employees who become overwhelmed with the demands of teamwork and innovation.

Sarason (1972) also emphasizes the creation, rather than the maturation, of settings. He writes, however, of barometric events that may signal decline: the departure of the leader, palliatives such as administrative reorganization, and boredom and discontent among members of the setting. These maladies are not inevitable, but they will occur if the predictable needs and problems of organizational creation are disregarded: "They are the realities that take some of the joy out of the honeymoon but make it more likely that a viable setting is being created" (Sarason, 1972, p. 128).

Because of the uncertainty surrounding the course of a mature organization, the final state of evolution has been characterized as one of "quasi-stationary equilibrium." This phrase is intended to convey the sense that the future state of an emergent organizational system is a dynamic one that cannot be precisely determined. Some organizations succeed and others fail. But there is reason to believe that the level of equilibrium realized in maturity—measured in terms of organizational effectiveness—will be directly affected by the skill with which developmental issues are negotiated in the critical first stages of growth.

COMMON PROPERTIES OF EMERGENT SOCIAL SYSTEMS

Any search for simple structure must avoid the pitfall of forcing complex empirical events into a simplistic, procrustean frame. But the theories we have cited suggest regularities in the development of nascent social systems. The pattern described by Sarason is, in many respects, similar to that identified by small group researchers, and that proposed by other organizational theorists. At a fundamental level, even Erikson's model of individual development appears similar in form.

The parallels are not perfect, and each theory is based on quite different sets of observations. But differences in the nature of the social organizations studied make the commonalities even more significant. Certainly, the convergence gives some support to Hartman and Gibbard's (1974b) contention that if one looks not only backward from the self-analytical group to the developing individual but also forward to larger societal processes, . . . analogies present themselves. The universal and political dilemma of man versus the state, of individualism versus group loyalty can be seen in similar fashion. It may be that political evolution and system maintenance—particularly nation building and the stabilizing of countries through time—replicate on a larger societal level both the small group and the individual process we have been discussing. (pp. 175–176)

The common processes that we have proposed are summarized in Table 2-1, which depicts five developmental stages and their defining characteristics. The first period is a formative time of hopeful naiveté, a "honeymoon" period in which the architects of new settings are typically blinded to internal contradictions and emerging problems. The exact way in which this stage closes will depend on the unique properties of the setting, but there is reason to believe that the utopian period will be halted by conflict between the leader and one or more key members of the organization. This struggle will find its resolution in the demarcation of power and authority. Either the renegade chief will be banished to another domain or, as Slater (1966) suggests, the "sacred king" may be dispatched by his murderous followers.

This stormy era can be expected to give way to a time of relative calm—a third period in the organizational life cycle marked by relief that the tension of earlier times has subsided. This hiatus is short-lived, however, since interpersonal issues among subordinate members have yet to be resolved. It is here that concern for scarce resources, the attention of the leader, and other previously unattended problems become salient.

Explanations for the onset of these events may vary. They include Bion's (1959) concept of "pairing"; an extension of the "pecking order" notion; a displaced sibling rivalry; or simple competition for limited resources. The cross-level similarities are particularly complex during this period; in fact, it is probably characterized by a number of complementary themes, all

Table 2-1 Stages of Organizational Growth

	Developmental Periods				
	Stage I Utopian Fantasy	Stage II Challenge to Authority	Stage III Resolution	Stage IV Intergroup Conflict	Stage V Quasi-Stationary Equilibrium
Characteristics	Unrealistic expectations and missionary zeal	Confrontation between leader and key members of the organization	Hiatus following leader–member conflict	Confrontation among individuals or subunits	Transition to maturity and steady state
Corresponding theories of development *Organizational*					
Greiner	Growth through creativity	Crisis of leadership	Growth through direction	Crisis of autonomy	Crisis of ?
Sarason	Myth of unlimited resources	—————— Organizational craziness —————→			Decline
Group					
Bennis and Shepard	Dependency–flight Counterdependence—flight	Resolution–catharsis	Enchantment–flight	Disenchantment–flight	Consensual validation
Hartman and Gibbard	Mystical fusion Deification	Revolt	Utopianism	Bisexuality	Messianism
Individual					
Erikson	Hope	Will	Purpose Competence	Fidelity Love	Care Wisdom

of which serve to foment interpersonal and interunit conflict.

We have described the final phase of creation as a quasi-stationary equilibrium, but it is less a stage of growth than the beginning of an uncertain maturity. Unlike an individual, whose life span is finite, larger social systems are capable of renewing their membership in the pursuit of institutional immortality. Characterizing this period is therefore a difficult task, and the literature on time-limited groups and individual growth provides little guidance.

Perhaps this final phase may find its greatest utility as a demarcation point for the beginning of the end of an emergent organization. As Kimberly (1980) observes, "birth and early development on the one hand, and institutionalization, on the other, are two relatively distinct chapters in the biography of an organization" (p. 41). Beyond this point, the mature organization's trajectory becomes less predictable, and for our purposes, even less interesting. Our conceptualization, however, suggests that the history recorded in this second chapter of maturity will be strongly influenced by the organization's success in traversing the four previous periods of growth.

THE QUESTION OF LOCOMOTION: WHY COMMONALITY?

There is a strong scientific tradition supporting the contention that analogies exist at multiple levels of biological organization. General system theory (Bertalanffy, 1968) provides numerous examples of system isomorphs and this framework has been influential in the field of organizational behavior (see Katz & Kahn, 1966).

At the same time, it would be premature to conclude that all of the parallels described in our model are manifestations of a common set of processes. Bertalanffy (1968) isolates three possibilities in the description of phenomena. At one level are analogies: superficial similarities corresponding neither in their causal factors nor relevant laws. At another level are homologies: present only when there exists a formal correspondence between the laws governing similarly behaving, yet different, systems. In the third level of explanation, the specific laws or functions governing the behavior of particular systems may be stated with precision. In our model, the existence of parallelism has been observed, and a simple structure appears to cut cross the three levels of analysis. The demonstration of logical homology must, however, be based on a more complete understanding of the causal mechanisms underlying each level of development.

Simple causal explanations of convergence in developmental schedules are not easy to find. Slater's (1966) psychodynamic interpretation of the leadership crisis is, for example, one perspective that might be invoked to explain the phenomenon. But an ethologist might see this struggle, and later conflicts, in terms of a dominance hierarchy.

Part of the difficulty in identifying and comparing mechanisms of change is that few developmental theories are, themselves, adequately developed. Most propose a series of empirically observed growth stages without fully elaborating the underlying causal forces.

Erikson, for example, says relatively little about the underlying pressures that cause an individual to move across his or her epigenetic matrix. Other theorists are more specific: Piaget, for example, invokes the concept of "equilibration" to explain the development of the child. The equilibration process propels the organism from one equilibrium state—that is, from one organized system of action—to another. This teleological model is believed to be fundamental to the ontogenesis of structures (Flavell, 1963), but there remain many unanswered questions about the equilibration process. Ginsburg and Opper (1969) contend that

> there is little direct evidence supporting Piaget's views on equi-
> libration . . . Piaget seems to offer a useful critique of traditional
> views of development, but has not sufficiently elaborated his
> own view, which is the equilibrium theory. (p. 179)

If the mechanisms of individual growth are relatively un-
charted, then our understanding of the ontogenetic forces that
drive groups is equally inchoate. It is one thing to know that
groups enter a utopian period because they are experiencing
dependency–flight behavior, and another to know precisely
why a small collection of individuals engages in any particular
behavior at a particular time. Said another way, what is the
real cause? Of course, one could always dig "deeper," and a
search for the ultimate cause would undoubtedly be quixotic.
Still, our lack of understanding about developmental forces is
troubling, and it inhibits the explication of any metatheory of
creation.

Some explanations have been offered for the existence of
parallelism, and they may serve as a starting point. For example, Erikson's (1968) contention that the human life cycle
and human institutions have evolved in a mutually supportive
association would lead us to expect some congruence. But this
explanation is not very helpful in explaining the unique features of any particular stage of growth.

Lacking clear guideposts, we may postulate that the initial
utopian period has its origins in an almost inevitable time of
naiveté. Just as the infant has had no opportunity to test the
limits of growth and competence, the new organization has yet
to face its challenges. Most importantly, it has yet to fail. The
hope of the child is further inspired by the dreams of parents,
and in groups and organizations the dreams of adults are
fueled by their leaders and fellow adventurers.

One might further speculate that the subsequent challenge
to authority arises from the collision of these initial hopes
with individual power needs. This explanation would probably
come closest to that of the ethologist, although attempts to

generalize from the behavior of other animals are not without problems (see Gould, 1980). Still, the child's need to test his will against that of adults can be verified by any armchair empiricist or parent; it is a consistent, predictable occurrence.

Similar challenges to the authority of a group leader or chief executive officer are also frequent, but probably not as inevitable. The likelihood of these conflicts may be moderated by a host of influences, for example: fear of reprisal; a social-ization process that substitutes passive–aggression for direct confrontation; and the availability of alternative targets for aggressive energy. Female colleagues have suggested that groups composed entirely of women are less likely to encounter this stage or, at least, that their internal conflicts are less intense.

Even if such a difference exists, it is still not clear whether this occurs because women are dispositionally less aggressive (Maccoby & Jacklin, 1974), or because they are socialized to avoid conflict, or both. And there is evidence that organizations composed of women are indeed capable of generating internal conflict over issues of power (Berg, 1977), so the contrast with male organizations—if it exists at all—may be one of degree. In any case, it appears that most systematic study will have to be done before the effects of sex differences can be stated with any certainty.

The emergence of a period of resolution following a struggle for power is, perhaps, less difficult to understand. Just as an individual requires sleep after an exhausting day, the devel-oping child needs an opportunity for integration after its strug-gle with parental will. Similarly, groups and organizations require time to heal after internal strife. They are composed of individuals who are tired both physically and emotionally, and that explanation may suffice.

The presence of a fourth period of intergroup conflict is more difficult to explain. In the developing child, conflicts with peers during adolescence are associated with unique biogenetic events that do not occur in groups and organizations. At least, they do not occur with such intensity.

At the same time, the "pairing fantasy" of Hartman and Gibbard's group schema is a sexual one, and there is no reason to believe that the emergence of a particular stage is tied to a single underlying cause. It may be, for example, that interpersonal conflicts arise from a mélange of sexual energy, pressure toward relational intimacy, and the continued working through of needs for individual dominance. These may not be precisely the same fuels that feed the fires of adolescence, yet there is no theoretical requirement that they be identical. Given our rudimentary understanding of emergent social systems, we would speculate that some such association exists.

The period of equilibrium is probably not so closely related. It is, in any case, a sort of portmanteau. The states of equilibria for an individual approaching old age, a university self-examination group nearing the end of semester, or an organization reaching maturity are likely to be quite different. There are some common features, of course. For example, fear and anticipation of loss are shared by both individuals and groups whose lives are drawing to a close. Organizations typically do not suffer the same fate, to which the reincarnation of the March of Dimes following the defeat of polio bears witness. It is probably most useful, therefore, to think of this period simply as a time of maturation, without expecting the same sort of synchrony that existed in earlier stages.

At Centerton, we saw only the beginning of equilibrium, but we observed its earliest days in considerable detail. In the next chapters we will move from this theoretical perspective to a recounting of the plant's history, tracing its evolution from inception to the edge of maturity.

PART TWO

HISTORY OF
CENTERTON

Chapter Three

The Setting and the Quality of Work Life Program

Crown Medical Specialties was founded in 1897 as a tiny operation in the back of a West Coast drugstore. It grew rapidly and by the early 1970s was a large, diversified company with approximately 4,000 employees, over 800 different products, and an annual sales volume of over $80 million. The company produced pharmaceutical and medical equipment, veterinary products, and fractionated human plasma; it also manufactured a few consumer items such as first aid kits and insect repellent lotions. The organization was headed by a president and an executive vice-president, with vice-presidents for marketing, manufacturing, finance, and research. Its manufacturing plants were located throughout the United States and in four other countries.

In 1971, the senior management of Crown Medical Specialties responded to pressures for increased production by electing to build a new plant rather than expand their existing facilities. Primarily for economic reasons, that is, the existence of inexpensive labor, the location selected was Centerton, a small

43

rural town in the southeastern part of the United States. During the early planning for the Centerton plant, recommendations from a long-standing consultant to the firm resulted in a commitment to structure it as a high involvement plant discussed in Chapter 1. Although the consultant had not been directly involved with these high involvement organizations, he was familiar with the successes reported by General Foods, Procter & Gamble, and other companies regarding their new plants. And he convinced Crown senior management that the Centerton plant was a prime candidate for this approach.

When this decision was made, Centerton was planned as a relatively simple, labor intensive facility that would produce disposable intravenous equipment. Changing market conditions, however, altered the preliminary plan. By early 1973, Centerton had been designated as a plasma fractionation facility. Although the plant's design was changed to accommodate the complex technology of plasma production, the decision to apply high involvement principles in the new plant remained unchanged.

During the early planning period, the consultant approached the Department of Labor for support in using the new Centerton plant to examine the results of efforts to create a high involvement work setting. The Department agreed to fund the project, on condition that an independent evaluation of the experience be conducted by the Institute for Social Research (ISR). Thus the project began.

In February 1973, a memorandum of agreement was prepared, formalizing the commitment by Crown Medical Specialties to design the new Centerton plant according to a philosophy of participative management and the principles of job enrichment. It further outlined the general functions of the Institute for Social Research and the funding and monitoring role to be played by the Department of Labor.

In brief, the agreement stated that the consultants would provide Centerton managers with background material regarding Quality of Work Life concepts as well as information about other companies that had successfully used participative management. The Personnel Manager was given a key role in developing plans for staffing and organizing the plant according to the intervention philosophy. The consultants were to work with him and other top Centerton managers in developing selection and training procedures for the new employees.

The agreement also detailed the responsibilities of the Institute for Social Research staff. They would periodically collect data on Centerton employees, using attitudinal surveys and direct observation. In addition, the researchers would be given access to Centerton's personnel and production data. Finally, both the Centerton management and the consultants agreed to allow the researchers access to the plant to observe employee behavior, working conditions, and consultant activities.

It was later agreed that two Crown Medical plants would be involved in the research. The Centerton plant, which will be described in the remainder of this chapter, would serve as the primary focus for the research and consulting activities. Another plant located in Baytown, a large urban area on the West Coast, was designated as the "comparison site." The Baytown plant was a large facility that manufactured a number of pharmaceutical and biomedical products, and included plasma production departments similar—but not identical—to those in the Centerton organization. Unlike Centerton, Baytown relied on older, but proven, equipment, and its employees had years of experience with the production process.

THE PLASMA TECHNOLOGY

Blood transfusions have been used in medical practice for many years. Before World War II, however, blood processing technologies were used only in research laboratories. In order to produce the large volume of plasma related products required by massive battle casualties, larger scale processing emerged during the war. Crown Medical Specialties was one of the several firms that responded to an invitation from the United States government to build plants that could use newly invented plasma processing methods. By the end of the war, the success of these plants made it clear that plasma proteins could be adapted to large scale production methods and made available for a wide range of medical uses. Today the amount of plasma processed in the United States is more than ten times greater than that produced during the war years.

The Centerton plant was designed to produce five plasma products: plasma protein fraction, albumin, tetanus immune globulin, immune serum globulin, and an anti-hemophiliac factor. Plasma processing is a highly complex and capital-intensive process that involves a sophisticated, proprietary technology. Three to five months are required from the receipt of plasma from U.S. donor centers to delivery of the final product.

The production process can be divided into three major steps. In the plasma pooling and fractionation operation, liters of frozen plasma are first thawed, pooled, and fractionated into their various components. Each plasma fraction is separated by the repeated application of chemical additives and temperature control. The separated plasma fractions are then processed through high speed, refrigerated centrifuges which precipitate the solid fraction from the remaining liquid. Each solid fraction is freeze-dried into powder form, and the liquid is further processed for the next fraction. Temperature in the fractionation room is maintained at $-5°C$ to prevent protein breakdown.

In the second major production operation, filtration and filling, plasma powder is dissolved in sterilized kettles and passed through an intricate filtration system. This process is carefully monitored and the plasma is subjected to numerous in-process tests. Each filtered batch is sampled and further tested for quality, after which it is sterile-poured into bottles, pasteurized, and incubated. The liquid bulk is then tested for protein and chemical concentration and poured into containers. The final major step, finishing, includes inspection, labeling, and boxing.

The products of this complicated process are subject to both the internal standards of Centerton's Quality Assurance Department and the standards of the Food and Drug Administration's Bureau of Biologics. Elaborate control systems are required to minimize error and thus ensure product safety. These include equipment for continuous monitoring of the process, testing built into the process itself, and testing conducted by the Quality Assurance Department.

In the final step of the process, biological, chemical, and other quality assurance tests are conducted. To monitor product sterility, potency, and pyrogenicity (the property of causing fevers in living organisms), seven biological tests are run. Approximately 25 chemical tests are performed to ensure purity of raw material and to measure the chemical concentrations of the product at various stages. Some 11 other inspections include tests for particulates in the products and general inspection of equipment involved in the final packaging operation (e.g., tubing, bottles, sealers, stoppers, labels, and cartons).

In such an exacting process, even minute errors can result in the loss of a batch worth thousands of dollars. Plasma products in powdered form are worth more than their weight in gold.

The delicacy of the process is accentuated by its craftlike nature. For a large number of functions, procedures are not specified to the point of routinization. Furthermore, the Centerton plant was based on a "state of the art" technology that was not yet supported by established written procedures. There was, therefore, ample room for errors within the production process, and mistakes at any point had serious implications for subsequent operations.

CENTERTON: THE RESEARCH SITE

Centerton is a small rural town 20 miles from the nearest substantial city, the state capital. The town is surrounded by two very different milieux. Not far to the north is an area with universities, laboratories, and research centers. Seaward of this cosmopolitan area, and toward the Centerton plant, the land changes into an agricultural region with a "Bible belt" culture. The plant itself was built on 77 acres of a former soybean field. Immediately surrounding the facility are tobacco and soybean fields; there are several small towns nearby.

The Centerton plant is one of several manufacturing concerns that have moved to the area in the past decade, taking advantage of low costs and the rarity of union activity. According to some staff members, the location was chosen for its accessible labor market, adequate railroad and trucking facilities, and its proximity to a large regional market.

The plant was welcomed by the local community. At the groundbreaking ceremonies in September 1972, the state governor, local civic leaders, and citizens turned out to hail the economic boost that the plant's multi-million dollar operation was expected to bring to the community.

The Organization

The plant is a large facility, representing an investment of over $10 million. As illustrated in Figure 3-1, it is composed of four separate buildings, each housing the organization's major subunits: Administration/Warehouse, Production, Quality Assurance Laboratories, and Engineering/Maintenance. The technical process largely dictated the plant's physical lay-

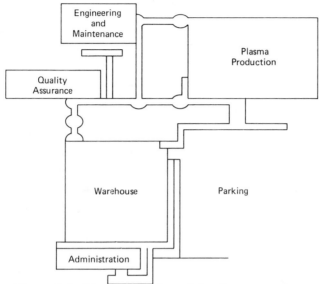

Figure 3-1   Physical design of the Centerton plant.

out; for the most part, the consultants did not contribute to its design.

Because absolute sterility is essential to plasma production, Centerton's physical layout was designed to minimize the danger of contamination. The production area is divided into "hot" (or sterile) and "cold" areas. To enter a hot area, workers must follow an elaborate double gowning procedure; to exit, they must shower and change out of the specially designed production clothing. The unusual attire resembles surgeons' garb, including face masks, head and shoe covers, and space suit style outfits for the refrigerated area. Workers use special equipment to sterilize materials brought into the hot production areas.

These provisions for sterility tend to minimize traffic between Centerton's hot and cold areas. Production workers tend to stay within the hot production areas throughout their shifts and usually do not have much contact with the front office. They do have regular contact, however, with other Centerton technicians, such as maintenance staff, who make periodic visits to the production area.

The Centerton plant was ultimately intended to house a facility that would produce plasma products, hospital equipment, and other assorted product lines. In its early days, however, the sole emphasis was on plasma production. By its fourth year of operation the plant was fully staffed with about 150 employees, about 20 percent of whom were managers or supervisors. The majority of Centerton employees were located in the Production and Quality Assurance departments. Supporting these two major departments were employees in the Engineering and Maintenance Department and two administrative departments—Personnel and Accounting.

Under the assumption of rapid growth, a relatively large management group was employed at start-up. The management was comprised of the Plant Manager and a manager for each major department—Plasma Production, Quality Assurance, Accounting, Engineering and Maintenance, and Personnel. In addition, the Production Department had two additional managers for Fractionation and Filtration.

In many ways, the Production and Quality Assurance Departments can be regarded as semi-independent organizations. The Production Department is responsible for production yields; the Quality Assurance Department is responsible for quality and compliance with federal standards. The two departments also have independent lines of authority. Production is headed by the plant manager, but to ensure the independence of monitoring activities, the Quality Assurance Department reports to the Quality Assurance division at the corporate level (Figure 3-2).

The Production Department is organized along functional lines. Its two major subdivisions are the Fractionation Unit

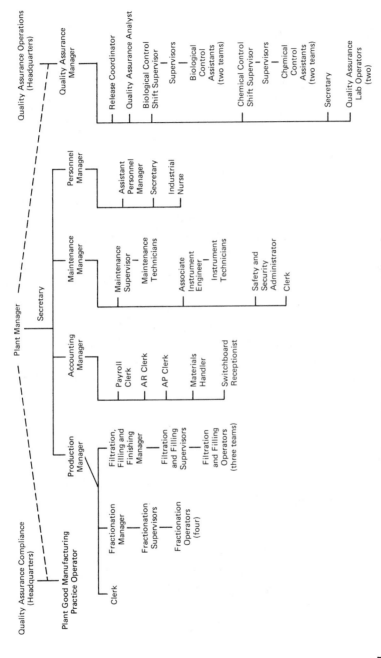

Figure 3-2 Centerton organizational structure.

and the Filtration, Filling, and Finishing Unit. In the Fractionation Unit, one team is responsible for pooling and one for Fractionation. Teams responsible for filtration and filling, and for product finishing, comprise the other unit.

The teams work on several schedules. Fractionation teams work 12-hour shifts (4 days one week; 3 days the next), rotating their day and night shifts. Filtration, pooling, and finishing teams, however, work on a fixed schedule. These teams also vary in size. Pooling, fractionation, and filtration teams consist of four to six individuals whereas finishing tasks are performed by a flexible team with five full-time and thirteen part-time operators.

The Quality Assurance Department comprises about a quarter of the plant population and a third of the managerial and supervisory personnel. It is divided into three sections: the biology laboratory, the chemical laboratory, and the inspection section. In addition, a coordinator reviews manufacturing and quality assurance documents and ensures that all regulations are met before the product is released.

The Engineering and Maintenance Department is responsible for servicing the complex refrigeration, steam, sterile water, and air systems necessary for production. It is also responsible for the maintenance and repair of the plasma processing machinery. Finally, the Accounting and Personnel departments perform the traditional administrative activities essential to any organization.

THE QUALITY OF WORK LIFE CONSULTANTS

Joining the consultant who had initiated the Centerton experiment were two other individuals who were to play active roles in the Quality of Work Life program. All three consultants were affiliated with a behavioral science consulting firm based in the West Coast. Although they functioned as a team, the consultants played very distinct roles in the Centerton's development.

The Project Director

The Project Director was a consulting and clinical psychologist. Over the past two decades, he had engaged in consultation with numerous organizations, including a police force and a plastics subsidiary of Crown Medical Specialties. Prior to his Centerton assignment, he had engaged in a broad range of organization development activities, which included Quality of Work Life programs and interventions designed to foster open communication and worker involvement in problem solving. The Project Director had extensive experience in providing individually focused psychological consultation to various client firms. He had often administered psychological tests and had provided personal evaluation and counseling in his consulting efforts. None of his work, however, had involved settings with Centerton's attributes: a new plant with a highly sophisticated and unpredictable technology.

The Project Director was responsible primarily for the inception of the program. He convinced the managers of Crown Medical Specialties, with whom he had had a long-standing advisory relationship, to design the new Centerton plant using behavioral science principles. He was the guiding force behind the intervention and was a continuing influence throughout the 3-year project.

Although the Project Director's contribution was greater at a conceptual level than in the day to day implementation of the program, he performed a number of critical functions. He coordinated the intervention team and maintained contact with top management at Centerton and corporate headquarters. The Project Director also had a significant influence on staffing decisions at Centerton through his psychological assessments of key managerial and supervisory personnel. He later had periodic contacts with managers and supervisors in psychological testing and counseling sessions, in consultations regarding interpersonal problems, and in workshops and seminar sessions held on participative management.

The Principal Investigator

The Principal Investigator had previously been affiliated with a private consulting firm established by the Project Director. He was a clinical psychologist who also did psychological consulting for manufacturing organizations and had previously worked with another Crown Medical plant. This organization was an established facility that produced hospital equipment of the sort Centerton was originally intended to manufacture. At this plant, which was having production problems, he served as a problem solving resource and communication facilitator, and was perceived as being instrumental in achieving greater openness and participation in the plant.

The Principal Investigator was the source of most of the day-to-day intervention activity at the beginning of the project. At the onset of the intervention, he worked intensively with the Plant Manager, the Personnel Manager, and other key managers and supervisors to instill basic concepts of participative management and job enrichment. To do this, the Principal Investigator combined a number of functions. He assisted in general planning, conducted workshops aimed at team building in upper management, designed the selection process, and facilitated interpersonal relationships. To many, he was "the authority" on participative management.

The Principal Investigator established unusual rapport and credibility with people at the Center plant. In the Personnel Manager's words, his personal style provided

> a model for desired behavior; his role, due to his personality,
> consultative style, and strong regard for a truly open and ethical
> approach to people and problems, contributed in large measure

to the success and good start developed in the initial training programs.

The Principal Investigator worked intensively on the project from May 1973 to May 1974, when he left for a scientific exchange program in the Soviet Union. He returned to Centerton in March 1975 and was present for the final stages of the intervention.

The Participant–Observer

When she first joined the consulting team, the Participant–Observer held a master's degree in management and was a graduate student in a program of clinical psychology. She began working on a part-time basis in November 1973 and worked on site full-time from mid-May 1974 until the end of June 1975.

An analysis of the Participant–Observer's role is crucial to understanding the nature of the intervention. The role evolved substantially, changing from one of "observer," whose purpose was data gathering, to that of "participant" with a major responsibility for intervention activities. Toward the end of the project, she returned to her original role and engaged in relatively little active intervention. The observer emphasis in the intended Participant–Observer role was reflected in an early proposal drafted by the change team:

> The Participant–Observer will focus on the dynamics of individual interventions, the process aspects of the utilization of behavioral science knowledge. Evaluation will be limited to assessing the impact of . . . interventions as revealed in direct observation of employee and management behavior.

In terms of Junker's (1960) categorizations, the Participant–Observer was to be an "observer as participant," an outsider whose primary function was to collect information. She was to be the historian of the consulting team, and her observations were intended to provide a rich and intensive data base for ongoing adjustment of the project and self-evaluation by the consultant team.

As time went on, however, the primary responsibility for carrying out the intervention was given to the Participant–Observer. This development was due, in part, to the Principal Investigator's departure for the Soviet Union. In addition, the Project Director's West Coast location and the constraints of his consulting budget made him relatively inaccessible to Centerton. For the most part, after the departure of the Principal Investigator, the on site Participant–Observer worked independently, communicating with the Project Director primarily by mail and telephone.

In the beginning, she provided consultation to the Personnel Manager on training needs and workshop planning. She also supplied feedback to individual managers who expressed interest in receiving comments on their interpersonal style—particularly the Quality Assurance and Production Managers. She also served as a catalyst for repairing interpersonal fences and for eliciting feelings that otherwise might have been suppressed. Occasionally, she attended team meetings, after which she would comment on the effectiveness of group participation or communication. Another of her major roles was that of "ombudsperson," serving as a channel of information outside the formal communication system of the organization. This aspect of the Participant–Observer's role became a quasi-managerial function, and she became highly involved in Centerton operations.

THE QUALITY OF WORK LIFE PHILOSOPHY

The consultants placed heavy emphasis on a management style that invited members' participation in matters that affected their lives. A letter from the consultants to the Department of Labor (September 22, 1973) said:

The basic concept underlying the consultation is participative management, involving a set-up wherein all employees are encouraged to express their suggestions, questions or criticisms pertaining to any aspect of the organization, design, structure, or administration of the work, and are given an opportunity to participate in the decision making process governing or affecting work arrangements.

According to the Principal Investigator, such a style increases the psychological meaningfulness of work and provides a foundation for other improvements in the design, structure, and organization of work.

Implementation of the principle of participation depended on a number of logical corollaries that then became intervention goals: adequate communication vertically and laterally, prompt and thoughtful response to suggestions provided, and in general, an environment that encouraged employee participation in decisions affecting their work or their personal lives.

In conjunction with the notion of participative management, the consultants focused their attention on the design of jobs. In contrast to many other plants in the pharmaceutical field, most tasks at Centerton were to be performed by work teams. Within these teams each individual's job was broadly defined and called for a variety of skills involving the production of a substantial portion of the product. As much as possible, responsibility was to be delegated by the supervisors to the team itself. This emphasis on job enrichment was to be integrated with the participative mandate to achieve the ultimate goals of high motivation and productivity in an enjoyable work situation.

The theoretical underpinnings of the intervention were traced by the consultants to two related branches in the literature of applied behavioral science: participation and job enrichment. McGregor's (1960) Theory Y, a theory of motivation and the nature of human beings, was a cornerstone of the participative philosophy. According to McGregor, work can be an important source of rewards to individuals if management arranges conditions so that people can achieve their own goals by directing their efforts toward organizational objectives. He proposed the concept of participative management as a vehicle for Theory Y beliefs: "Participation, which grows out of the assumptions of Theory Y, offers substantial opportunities for ego satisfaction for the subordinate and thus can affect motivation toward organizational objectives" (1960, p. 130).

Participation is hypothesized to have positive effects on individual satisfaction, motivation, and ultimately, productivity. One proposition suggests that participation is in itself intrinsically satisfying, and that engaging in the decision making process is both enjoyable (Tannenbaum, 1966) and enhancing to one's self-importance and self-esteem (Strauss, 1963). Another proposition suggests that participation is motivating because workers become "ego involved" in decisions they help make (Vroom & Yetton, 1973; Yukl, 1971) and are then more motivated to carry them out. In addition to these benefits, it has been suggested that participation results in better decisions or better products, since the workers closest to the problems in their jobs know best how to solve them (Miles, 1965), and that participation taps the latent creativity, responsibility, and abilities of the workers (Singer, 1974). The consultants used these ideas as the bases for their training programs.

Unlike participative management, job enrichment is a relative newcomer to the field of work improvement. The basic theories of job enrichment used by the consultants can be traced to statements by Herzberg (1966), Turner and Lawrence (1965), Hackman and Lawler (1971), and Hackman and Oldham (1974). In essence, the theory states that positive outcomes, both personal and work related, result from critical psychological states obtained when certain characteristics are present in a person's job.

Hackman and Oldham (1974) propose a three-step process in which key job characteristics—variety, autonomy, identification with task, feedback, and task significance—lead to three psychological states. These critical states—experienced mean-

ingfulness, responsibility for outcomes, and knowledge of results—in turn produce a set of desired motivational effects.
These outcomes, which can be expected when individuals with
strong needs for growth are given enriched jobs, include high
motivation, high quality of work performance, high job satisfaction, and low absenteeism and turnover.

As was true with participation, the consultants began with
previous theoretical work in their introduction of job enrichment to the Centerton plant. They trained the managers in its
principles and introduced them to other companies that were
applying job design ideas on the shop floor. In their intervention work, however, they actually placed more emphasis on
team organization than on the individual job enrichment approaches described by Herzberg, Hackman, and others. Opportunities for job redesign were limited by the nature of the
technology and, indeed, the social system seemed more amenable to intervention than did the plasma production technology.

A third element of the consultants' philosophy was a clinical
counseling orientation that focused on individual traits, abilities, and personal styles. Their consultation used two related
approaches: intensive psychological evaluation and testing, to
be used for personnel selection and individual self-awareness;
and training in behavioral styles beneficial to the employees'
own growth as well as their capacity to function effectively
within a participative environment.

Individual counseling and training were thought to provide
the support and guidance needed to deal with an unfamiliar
and often difficult work situation. For many managers and
supervisors accustomed to operating within relatively traditional management structures, a considerable amount of "un-
learning" was required. And an even greater amount of new
learning was needed to negotiate a loosely structured and open
management system. Much of this reeducation was to be acquired in an individual and experiential mode through interaction with, and feedback from, the consultants.

THE QUALITY OF WORK LIFE INTERVENTION METHODOLOGIES

The consultants engaged in a wide range of activities during the course of the intervention. We have classified these methods as follows: exposition and propagation; interpersonal feedback; testing and counseling; behavioral modeling; on-call consultation; survey feedback; and information channeling. Each will be reviewed briefly.

Exposition and Propagation

This educational approach, considered by Bennis (1966) to be the most popular method generally used in organizations, was the primary strategy employed by the intervention team. The technique of exposition and propagation assumes that knowledge leads to sophistication in rearranging social systems or making strategic organizational interventions (Bennis, 1966). This approach was exemplified by the early exposure of Centerton's top managers to organization development principles as well as the formal training sessions held for the managers, supervisors, operators, and technicians.

The Plant and Personnel Managers were given special orientation to these concepts through conversations with the consultant, exposure to literature, and contact with organizations operating with Quality of Work Life principles. The rest of the managerial and supervisory staff was provided with two workshops on Quality of Work Life concepts, particularly participation and job enrichment. These workshops, conducted jointly by the Project Director and the Principal Investigator, had a social-psychological and interpersonal emphasis and focused on such areas as group dynamics, leadership style and interpersonal feedback. These sessions employed a combination of teaching methods, including readings and lectures on participative management, motivation, and resistance to change;

case studies; movies; and small group problem solving discussions and critiques. The Personnel Manager, aided by the Participant–Observer and the Project Director, conducted similar training workshops for nonsupervisory employees; these are discussed further in the following chapter. Relatively little emphasis was placed on managerial visits to existing high involvement plants. Of course, at this point in time, few existed, and some of the ones that did—for example, the Procter & Gamble plants—were not open to visitors.

Interpersonal Feedback

A major share of the intervention effort focused on the interpersonal processes of Centerton employees. These consulting activities were not so much aimed at specific changes as they were intended to create relationships that facilitated decision making and collaboration. The Principal Investigator, at the start, and the Participant–Observer, in the later part of the intervention, worked to improve interpersonal communication both at the individual and group level. These activities frequently took the form of providing feedback to individuals regarding their behavior and its "fit"—or lack of fit—with the philosophy of the program. For the most part, this help was given only when specifically requested by an employee.

Testing and Counseling

Traditional industrial psychological consultation was provided in several forms by the Project Director and the Principal Investigator. At the very beginning of the project, psychological testing of prospective supervisors was conducted to identify individuals who would be able to function well in an organization with a participative management philosophy. Counseling on personality styles and work behavior was later provided to key managers and supervisors after they had been hired.

Behavioral Modeling

In this approach the behavior of the consultant is the instrument of change: his or her own actions are employed as a teaching tool. The impact of behavioral modeling depends as much on the credibility of the model as on actual behaviors. Owing in part to the unusual rapport he had created, the Principal Investigator served as the major role model in the Centerton effort. Because of the infrequency of the Project Director's visits to Centerton, it was less feasible for him to function in this role. The Participant–Observer served, to a lesser extent, as a role model for participative management. But for reasons to be detailed later, she was limited in her ability to establish the same level of rapport as the Principal Investigator, and thus used this modality less successfully.

On-Call Consultation

The consultants were available to assist in the planning process at various stages of Centerton's development. As previously mentioned, the Project Director had consulted with the management of Crown Medical Specialties on Quality of Work Life issues before the new plant was established, and was influential in the decision to implement a participative management style at Centerton. The most direct and intensive consultations occurred at the very beginning, when the Principal Investigator worked with the Personnel Manager and the supervisors to specify criteria and procedures for the initial recruitment and selection efforts. During later stages, the Participant–Observer worked closely with the Personnel Manager in devising training workshops for new employees.

Members of the consulting team were also available to assist with the problems encountered in applying Quality of Work Life concepts to organizational operating problems. The consultants' strategy here was to wait for consulting requests rather than to initiate projects of their own. As time progressed, however, relatively little use was made of this on-call consultation service.

Survey Feedback

Survey feedback involves the systematic use of diagnostic data for the purpose of achieving organizational change. The consultants made some attempts to use the questionnaire data provided by the Institute for Social Research as part of the research effort. Responses from a short attitudinal questionnaire were plotted each month, at first by the Participant–Observer and later by a member of the Personnel Department. For a period of time, monthly departmental results were posted as "ISR Information Centers" in the Production and Maintenance areas.

In addition, the Participant–Observer prepared a verbal summary of the results from a longer assessment questionnaire administered in November 1974. The report was made available to managers and supervisors who were then left to disseminate or discuss the document as they saw fit. Although no further action was taken by most of the department managers, a summary of the document was discussed in two sessions by the Quality Assurance Department.

Information Channeling

This activity was performed primarily by the Participant–Observer, who acted as an "information conduit" independent of formal organizational mechanisms. This involved, for example, alerting managers and supervisors to existing or potential problems in their own departments, as well as providing them with information about developments in other parts of the organization.

SUMMARY

The Centerton Quality of Work Life program was initiated in a new organization distinguished by its sophisticated, proprietary technology. The consultants had little prior experience with this kind of organization, but they were able to introduce a number of features that typify high involvement work settings: self-managing teams, a participative management style, job enrichment, and a collaborative selection system designed to choose individuals who were compatible with the participative philosophy.

The consultants employed a number of approaches in implementing the program, including considerable on site teaching, personal counseling, and in some cases, actually performing management functions in a quasi-official capacity. The intensity of these activities changed over the course of the intervention. The program began with a high level of activity, but diminished in intensity as the intervention moved toward completion.

Chapters 4 and 5 describe the unfolding of these events, which are summarized at the conclusion of Chapter 5 with a calendar that details critical milestones in the history of the Centerton plant.

Chapter Four

Centerton's Early Days: The Promise of Utopia

Shortly after ground was broken for the Centerton plant in late 1972, the consultants began to work with key managers, most of whom had been transferred from other Crown plants. Through extensive conversations and exposure to companies implementing similar programs, the consultants propagated Quality of Work Life ideas among the Centerton managers.

Commitment to the Quality of Work Life philosophy was an essential characteristic of Centerton managers in those early days. Although the management team members had differing opinions about the meaning of the Quality of Work Life program, it was clear from the start that Centerton was to be a high involvement plant. In fact, the Project Director had been involved in many of the original staffing decisions.

The Plant Manager had previously managed another Crown plant. Although relatively unfamiliar with the literature of participative management, he had successfully used its basic principles to deal with some thorny union problems. A pragmatist, he appreciated the benefits a Quality of Work Life philosophy could bring to a production facility.

The Production Manager had been recruited from the Baytown plant and was also a longtime Crown Medical employee. His extensive technical experience, however, was not matched by managerial expertise. He characterized himself as a member of the old school of autocratic management and he anticipated having to make a real effort to adjust to the participative ideology at Centerton.

The Quality Assurance Manager was also from the Baytown plant. Although he was unfamiliar with the new management style, its basic concepts appealed to him from the beginning. Because his staff was well educated with advanced technical expertise, he was sure that participative management would work well in his department.

The Personnel Manager, hired in January 1973, completed the top team. His previous positions had prepared him to deal with traditional personnel concerns, such as hiring, designing employee benefit packages, and training. Like the other managers, he was unacquainted with many of the behavioral science concepts espoused by the consultants. In the program design, however, he was expected to play a pivotal role, merging the Quality of Work Life implementation efforts with his more traditional personnel duties.

SUPERVISOR SELECTION

Procedures for staffing the remainder of the plant began immediately after Centerton's core management team was complete. Consultation was provided during this period almost exclusively by the Project Director, who had developed close working relationships with the Centerton managers—particularly the Personnel Manager. In addition to providing them with the general principles of the Quality of Work Life philosophy, he was a key figure in the design of the initial selection and training procedures.

The Project Director and Personnel Manager together drew up a list of attributes with which to select employees. For managers and supervisors, these personality characteristics included the following:

1. Maturity: Manages own emotions and feelings effectively and is aware of and responsive to those of others.

2. Interest in others: A genuine interest and respect for the ideas and feelings of others.

3. The ability to act as coach or coordinator: To relinquish the traditional supervisory authority.

Managers and supervisors were expected to have the ability to focus on work related problems, to understand the functions and relationships of Centerton's departments, to realistically appraise external requirements, and to be action oriented. Nonsupervisory employees, likewise, were expected to have personality characteristics compatible with the participative management style—basic friendliness, flexibility, maturity, high sociability, adequate intelligence, good social communication skills, and desirable work related attitudes (such as the desire to learn, the desire to take responsibility, and dependability).

Although the consultants were available to the entire Centerton team, Quality of Work Life activities in the early days centered on the Production Department. The Project Director and Principal Investigator helped the Production Manager select the supervisors in charge of the fractionation and filtration processes. The Fractionation Manager they chose was an experienced Baytown employee. Although the consultants expressed some reservations about his flamboyant managerial style and previous "personality conflicts" with the Production Manager, he was transferred to Centerton because of his technical expertise. The Filtration Manager, in contrast, was hired on the basis of potential rather than experience. Despite his lack of management experience, he was thought to meet the criteria for a good Centerton manager.

Supervisory selection began in August 1973. The consultants worked with key managers to select the first seven production supervisors. Supervisory applicants were given psychological tests, including the Closure Flexibility Test (Thurston & Jeffrey, 1959) and the Rosenzweig Picture Frustration Test (Rosenzweig, 1945), to identify individuals who could both deal with a participative management philosophy and tolerate the frustrations of start-up. Most of the supervisors chosen were young, idealistic, and inexperienced. One manager later said:

> We hired with an objective. Here we had a long-term growth situation. We hired a lot of young people with academic training and the [right] mentality, flexible and not set in their ways. But we, in my opinion, missed an essential ingredient: we did not have enough experience in the group.

To some extent, the managers chose inexperienced people because a large pool of experienced, available candidates did not exist. But the selections also reflected a deliberate strategy. A new plant needed fresh approaches, and the managers and consultants feared that longtime employees might resist nontraditional methods. In any case, the group of supervisors ultimately selected lacked firsthand experience with the technology. The Plant Manager said:

> You always have a trade-off—you get the experience and trade off the [necessary] attributes, and you run the risk that people are so ingrained and so inflexible in their thinking they can't accept change. You go the other way, you get what we got.

"What they got" they quickly exposed to participation and team building. In October 1973, the consultants and the Personnel Manager conducted two three-day workshops for the Centerton managers and supervisors. These workshops presented the basic tenets of participative management, motivation, communication, and team functioning. Through large and small group discussions, movies and short lectures, the Centerton staff became familiar with the language of social science as applied to management—Herzberg's two-factor theory of motivation, McGregor's "Theory X and Theory Y," and the concepts of "higher and lower order needs." Excitement and exchange were high during these sessions as the Centerton team began to embrace the mission of their new plant.

THE SELECTION OF PRODUCTION OPERATORS

The supervisors applied their new skills in the first weeks of January 1974, when they selected the Centerton production operators. They used procedures similar to those adopted by the Topeka General Food plant (Walton, 1972). In December, the consultants conducted a three-day workshop for supervisors to learn interviewing techniques. Shortly afterward, the core team (the supervisors, the Personnel Manager, and the Principal Investigator) developed interviewer evaluation scales. These scales consisted of seven items on which applicants were rated from zero ("unsatisfactory") to eight ("outstandingly good"). The items were:

1. Experience, training, relevant knowledge, skill; probable value of previous experience, special training and know-how in his areas of supposed capability.

2. Motivation for the job: Why did he come to the organization? Does he seem dependable? Will he invest himself in the job and strive to perform excellently?

3. Ability to listen understandingly, interest in others, ability to attend and follow another's ideas.

4. Appearance, cleanliness, dress, looks, posture, and physique.

5. Communication skills: enunciation, grammar, language facility, voice quality, coherence in expressing self.

6. Compatibility and self-confidence: impact in contacting people, readiness to smile, sincerity, graciousness, courtesy, tact.

7. Attitude.

The team also developed the following advertisement, which was placed in local newspapers:

CROWN MEDICAL SPECIALITIES
CENTERTON PLANT
NEEDS PRODUCTION WORKERS
To be Trained for Plasma Processing Technicians

Work in new, modern plant (producing vital, life-saving medical products) with an exciting new style of supervision and management which will allow you to participate and work in jobs which emphasize individual potential, learning, responsibility, and decision-making.

QUALIFICATIONS:
1. High School graduate (or the equivalent).
2. Completion of science courses such as: Chemistry, Biology, Math, or Physics.
3. Production work experience in a manufacturing plant is desirable.
4. Mechanical aptitude.
5. Willing to accept greater responsibility and learn new skills in broader jobs.
6. Willing to work rotating shifts (including some weekends with days off during week).
7. Desire to work as member of a team.

If you meet these qualifications and would like to be a part of a company that emphasizes individual potential, learning and responsibility, with excellent earnings and benefits, please come and see us.

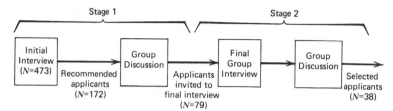

Figure 4-1   Steps in the selection process.

More than 400 applicants responded to this advertisement, and interviews were conducted in January 1974. The interview process consisted of two stages (see Figure 4-1). During the initial interview, supervisors established basic qualifications and evaluated the candidates according to the seven criteria developed by the Principal Investigator and the Centerton staff. Each supervisor then recommended the most promising candidates to a meeting of supervisors. The complete set of supervisors then selected the candidates who would receive final interviews.

The final interviews were conducted by the same group of supervisors in addition to the managers of the two major sub-units, Fractionation and Filtration. These interviews were used to clarify the applicants' qualifications, such as team experience and scientific background, and to discuss such issues as pay and work requirements. Finally, the interviews probed dimensions considered important to the management philosophy, such as sources of life fulfillment, ability to work with people, personal and job goals, and on-the-job learning experiences. Applicants were also asked questions about their outside interests and family. Following this final interview, members of the two departments met separately to debate the merits of the applicants and to make final decisions.

Out of an initial pool of 473 applicants, 38 were finally selected. Later comparisons of the supervisor's ratings of both the selected and rejected applicants indicated that factors relevant to job success (e.g., ability and knowledge) seemed to be given relatively little weight in the selection decisions. The greatest difference in test ratings between selected and rejected applicants involved the "ability to listen understandingly," with the selected applicants scoring much higher on this factor. This result was unexpected; later interviews suggested that the importance placed on this factor may have resulted from the supervisors' participation in a workshop stressing trust, openness, interpersonal skills, and compatibility with Centerton's participative philosophy.

Our analysis of the Pre-Employment Questionnaire also indicated that candidates selected for jobs tended to be less concerned with their relationships at work than those not selected. Since the team structure is a key element of the Quality of Work Life philosophy, this finding was rather surprising. Further analyses suggested that this outcome may have resulted from the interviewers' tendency to choose applicants with characteristics similar to their own. Evidently, the supervisors—like their newly selected subordinates—did not place a particularly high value on work relationships. They were, as the Plant Manager later commented, individualistic "superstars"—aggressive, energetic, and unaccustomed to collaborative work. Whether this failure to value work relationships reflected a lack of ability in dealing with work colleagues is another question. But it does appear that the supervisors acted on a need to choose people similar to themselves; they considered relatedness needs to be of secondary importance.

Although the applicants finally selected may not have been the most suitable for a group-centered style of management, they were clearly the supervisors' own choices, and a spirit of camaraderie quickly developed within the teams. In addition, the nature of the selection process strengthened the supervisors' belief that the participative ideal could indeed be realized in the plant. (For a more complete discussion of the selection procedures and analyses, see Nieva, Perkins, & Lawler [1978, 1980].)

OPERATOR INTRODUCTION TO THE QUALITY OF WORK LIFE PROGRAM

Each applicant for the position of production operator had been given an introductory handout which presented the plant in idealized terms. The Centerton plant, according to the handout, would be manufacturing the best and safest lifesaving products that modern science could create. Centerton extolled Quality of Work Life principles in these handouts:

> We will work together in a team atmosphere. . . . In the Centerton plant you will have opportunities to express yourself and to participate in decisions and matters which affect you. You will find that this will create more interest in your job, more satisfaction and a feeling of accomplishment which accompanies a vital, worthwhile job. Our jobs will be much broader and less routine than any other manufacturing plant in this area because we work together in a team-work manner. Since we spend most of our waking hours working, we aim to set our jobs up so that we can get the most satisfaction out of them and enjoy doing them.

The new employees' training program, held from February 25 to March 7 of 1974, reinforced the message. The Plant Manager set the tone in his welcoming address: He spoke of creating a plant with an atmosphere in which people felt free to express themselves, where there would be communication "up, down, and sideways," where collective wisdom would be recognized as better than individual problem solving, and where a spirit of teamwork and cooperation would prevail. He posed the challenge of creating something different "through hard work in one big team." The Personnel Manager echoed the participative tone, stressing the uniqueness of the plant's philosophy and emphasizing the mutuality of the learning process: "You will not be criticized for telling us about our mistakes; they are inevitable." The Personnel Manager also emphasized Centerton's concern for the quality of work life at the plant, and the important role that the work groups' collective wisdom would play in operational decisions.

The training program introduced the new employees to Centerton's personnel policies and to the plant's basic technical operations. In the morning sessions, lectures, slide shows, and demonstrations focused on manufacturing practices and quality assurance techniques. Afternoons were devoted to team training sessions conducted by the Personnel Manager and the consultants.

These sessions were designed to provide the employees with both a conceptual framework and an opportunity to develop skills in group participation, leadership, and problem solving. In a typical session, a group would watch a film on communication in a work setting and then, under the leadership of a supervisor, discuss the problems likely to arise, such as the equity of rewards and incentives for employees, or discipline policies. These training teams were intended to "begin to build norms of open communication, self and others' critique, and personal involvement in all aspects of work life at Centerton" (Consultant Progress Report, 1974). Like the training sessions for the managers and supervisors, these programs emphasized interpersonal processes. The schedule of activities for the new employees training program is shown in Table 4-1.

Both supervisors and production operators reacted enthusiastically to these training sessions. The supervisors, especially, expressed strong positive feelings about their own and their subordinates' participation. Supervisors also positively assessed their own abilities as teachers, and perceived the new employees to be highly trainable—a determination they considered to be a confirmation of their hiring decisions. In short, the supervisors found their introduction to the roles of team leaders and technical trainers a heady experience.

Some of this enthusiasm reflected the general eagerness for start-up. The production supervisors and managers formed a highly cohesive and energetic group. The principles they had acquired appeared to work well—communication was frequent and open, and tentative experiments in self-expression appeared to have been accepted by management. The climate of trust and flexibility in Centerton's preproduction days seemed to provide a nearly ideal setting in which to practice new behaviors. And the Project Director provided an exceptionally competent role model for the novices in Quality of Work Life management.

Although the consultants tended to focus on the production staff, the idealism of the Production Department was shared by employees in Quality Assurance. To a large extent, this commitment can be attributed to the Quality Assurance Manager's personal emphasis on openness and communication. In fact, to some in the organization, he was giving participation too much emphasis. In the words of one manager, the Quality Assurance Manager "wanted to give the store away." If he did, his staff members were eager to take it. Mostly young and well educated, they took to the participative style immediately.

STRAINS IN UTOPIA

Although spirits were generally high during this time, it would be misleading to suggest that Centerton had no problems in its early days. For example, an early confrontation between the Personnel Manager and the production supervisors made it clear that operational schedules could interfere with the ideals of participative management. The incident occurred after Production and Quality Assurance managers and supervisors had spent a month at Crown headquarters for technical training. In their absence, the Personnel Manager had begun preparations for operator recruitment and selection. This initiative frustrated the supervisors, who felt that their telephoned suggestions had been disregarded.

Table 4-1 Crown Medical Specialities—New Employee Training Program Outline

Monday, Feb. 25, 1974	Orientation — Plasma fractionation operators and other new employees
8:00 AM–8:30 AM	Reception — Coffee and doughnuts
8:30 AM–9:30 AM	Welcome and introduction to Centerton
9:30 AM–10:15 AM	Review of benefit program and pay policies
10:15 AM–10:30 AM	Coffee break
10:30 AM–11:30 AM	1. Review of basic policies and procedures
	2. Plant facilities
	3. Safety procedures
11:30 AM–12:00 Noon	Summary
	1. What you can expect from Centerton
	2. What Centerton expects from you
	3. Review of schedule for balance of training program
12:00 PM–12:30 PM	Lunch
12:30 PM–1:30 PM	Plant tour
1:30 PM–2:00 PM	Completion of necessary payroll personnel forms by new employees
2:00 PM–4:30 PM	Technical training — Plasma fractionation operators; On-the-job training — Other employees
Tuesday–Friday, Feb. 26–March 1, 1974	
8:00 AM–4:30 PM	Technical training — Plasma fractionation operators; On-the-job training — Other employees
Monday, March 4, 1974	
8:00 AM–2:00 PM same schedule as Feb. 25	Orientation — Plasma filtration and filling operators and other new employees
2:00 PM–4:30 PM	Team training workshop — All employees
Tuesday, March 5, 1974	Good Manufacturing Practice (GMP)
8:00 AM–10:00 AM	1. Introduction to quality assurance procedures and systems
	2. Plant GMP and procedures auditor functions

	3. Introduction to GMP
10:00 AM–10:15 AM	4. Specific GMP requirements
10:15 AM–12:15 PM	Coffee break
	Quality Assurance
	1. Biological contamination
	2. Environmental contamination
12:15 PM–2:45 PM	Team training workshop
2:45 PM–3:00 PM	Break
3:00 PM–4:30 PM	Team training workshop

Wednesday, March 6, 1974

8:00 AM–10:00AM	Quality Assurance — Physical (raw material) testing
10:00 AM–10:15 AM	Break
10:15 AM–12:15 PM	Quality assurance — Chemical testing
12:15 PM–12:45 PM	Lunch
12:45 PM–4:30 PM	Technical training (OJT) (or possibly continuation of team training workshops)

Thursday, March 7, 1974

8:00 AM–10:00 AM	Quality Assurance
	1. Biological contamination
	2. Environmental contamination
10:00 AM–10:15 AM	Break
10:15 AM–12:15 PM	Good Manufacturing Practices
	1. Continuation of GMP requirements
	2. GMP requirements via flow of material
	3. FDA Film "No Margin for Error"
12:15 PM–12:45 PM	Lunch
12:45 PM–4:30 PM	Technical training (OJT, or possibly continuation of GMP)

Their hostility had been obvious at the beginning of the 3-day interviewing workshop in December, and some had questioned Centerton's commitment to its management philosophy—and even the validity of the philosophy itself. It was not until the Principal Investigator intervened that a frank discussion cleared the air enough for substantive training to begin. The confrontation led to a revision of the Personnel Manager's recruitment plan, which had proposed that the Personnel Department take the lead both in designing a system for recruitment and selection and in the initial screening of job applicants. The modification granted supervisors a greater role in designing the program and in developing the selection criteria and specific questions.

Another of the plant's early problems concerned the difficulty of maintaining both high performance standards and a spirit of camaraderie. A serious crisis arose when one of the original production supervisors had difficulty mastering the technical aspects of his job. Although other supervisors were equally lacking in relevant experience, this man had unusual trouble with the basic production concepts and techniques, even after heavy support from his manager and co-supervisors. His shortcomings were apparent when he was expected to lead and teach his team members. The Plant Manager's decision to terminate him was reached with much anguish. At the time his problems began, there were only 15 people at Centerton, all of whom worked very closely together. The others felt his termination almost as deeply as if they had rejected a member of the family.

Implementation of Centerton's vision of participative management was also damaged by external events. In February 1974, Crown Medical Specialties was purchased by a European firm. The new owners expected the plant to lift the company out of its severe financial difficulties, and the corporate headquarters subjected Centerton to increased surveillance. Perhaps even more important, the purchase raised uncertainty about whether Centerton's management philosophy would be acceptable to the new corporate leadership. Thus the new Centerton employees were being introduced to the plant's Quality of Work Life program at the same time that questions were being raised about corporate acceptability, and the meaning and application of the fundamental concept of participation. Reflecting this basic confusion, the Plant Manager deliberately dropped the phrase "participative management" from his welcoming address to the new employees. Privately, he explained that eliminating the rhetoric of participation did not imply diminished commitment to the concept. His stated rationale was that the deleted term had been used indiscriminately and had thereby lost its meaning. Subsequently, behavioral science terms like group problem solving and teamwork were substituted for the terminology of participative management. He also considered the use of less global language to be a way of combating unrealistic expectations regarding participation during the start-up period.

The Plant Start-Up

Plasma processing was originally scheduled to begin in March 1974. However, inexperienced personnel and equipment failure resulted in repeated scheduling delays, which led to a dampening of excitement and zeal. In these early days, Centerton had many of the problems common to new organizations—long working hours, new staff, machine breakdowns, and intense pressure. The challenge of mastering a nonroutine production technology was made more difficult by the balky equipment, much of which had been designed specifically for the Centerton plant. Technological malfunction was frequent before unfamiliar elements in the new equipment were debugged. The undependable refrigeration system caused continual problems and expensive product losses. A bottle washing system had to be replaced. Numerous batches had to be reprocessed because of sanitation and contamination problems.

These technological problems created difficulties for many of the new operators. Malfunctions created extended periods of forced inactivity, particularly for the filtration operators. To fill the time, the employees were put to work cleaning and scrubbing; this created more frustration and resentment.

Equipment problems were compounded by a lack of technically competent personnel. Of the seven initial supervisors, for example, only one had previous experience in plasma production, and only three had previous experience in any type of pharmaceutical production. In addition, Centerton's Maintenance and Engineering Division could not provide adequate technical backup for production, and it was difficult to obtain sufficient and timely access to corporate research and development personnel.

Adding to the demands of the internal situation at Centerton were pressures from outside the plant. Because of Centerton's financial importance to corporate headquarters, pressure to speed up the production schedule was extremely high. Many managers and supervisors felt that the production schedule gave them too little time to work through the technical and human problems accompanying start-up.

For managers and supervisors especially, workdays were extremely long. Not even their 12- to 16-hour days, however, were sufficient; Centerton's start-up problems seemed endless. The Plant Manager had a particularly difficult role, trying to get more out of his employees, even as he recognized what they were putting in. As he saw it: "People were doing their level best, working 60, 70, 80 hours a week. Even though the result, in my opinion, was not good, I could not sit down with that individual and say, 'You need improvement.'"

Centerton processed its first batch of plasma in June 1974. The celebration of this event temporarily broke the frustration and anger that had built up with each postponement of the start-up date. The elation, however, was short-lived. Work hours lengthened, tension increased, and the strain of meeting production demands started to affect Centerton workers when they were off the job. Even the Plant Manager, who was known to speak frequently of the need for personal sacrifices, started to talk about the excessive costs of start-up:

> The price gets too high; there are large strains on personal lives, on the family, and when there are children it gets worse. Wives come here—they have no relatives, close friends, and the husband is away all the time.

Internal production pressures were exacerbated by the new corporate emphasis on cost cutting. Many of the measures in themselves were trivial—for example, cafeteria services were reduced, orders for replacement materials were ignored, and free coffee was eliminated. But some, like delays in wage increases, were not. In combination, they took their toll on employee morale. As one manager commented:

> All the cost-saving measures—postponing raises for a year, cutting free coffee, cafeteria reduced, difficulty in replacing materials—Crown Medical is cutting its own throat. Saving $2,000 from the cafeteria is nothing compared to company morale.

In addition to these measures, Crown headquarters increased its pressure on the plant. Visits from headquarters were frequent, and the employees, particularly the managers, became apprehensive about the constant surveillance. Reports of major personnel changes at both the Baytown plant and at the corporate level made many of the Centerton employees uneasy.

Pressures were greater in the Production Department than in Quality Assurance. The laboratory technology in the Quality Assurance Department was complex, but not as novel and unpredictable as in Production. Furthermore, the majority of the Quality Assurance technicians had either formal training or work experience directly related to their jobs. In addition, the Quality Assurance Department as a whole had a lighter responsibility during the start-up period. Although the Department was charged with assuring product purity, Production had to manufacture the product in the first place. Similarly, Quality Assurance bore a lighter financial burden—if tests were not done properly, retesting was not excessively expensive. Production mistakes were vastly more costly and rectifying them was time-consuming.

As production uncertainties mounted, the Quality Assurance Manager played a significant role in shielding his staff from the turbulence. His technical expertise and independent line of authority probably enhanced his ability to act as a buffer: Because he reported to the corporate Quality Assurance Manager rather than the Plant Manager, he displayed a great deal of autonomy within the Centerton plant. And he used this autonomy to protect his subordinates from demands that he considered unreasonable. He once said: "The pressure stops with me—I don't pass it on—I stand up and fight. If things are not possible, I say so. We have to be realistic."

Problems with Participative Management

Although the new employees had received training in the concepts of participative management, it became evident soon after start-up that implementation would not be easy. "Participation" was understood by many employees as a mandate to involve everyone in every aspect of decision making. These efforts at universal participation frequently met with disappointment, but Centerton employees still aspired to the philosophy they believed the consultants had endorsed. One supervisor cited an example:

> We were holding meetings on everything. Things had to be changed because we couldn't function that way . . . one frac-

tionation team decided that the break room was not satisfactory. They wanted a color TV, and the supervisor carried it up the line to [the Production Manager]; [the request] was finally turned down. Things were all so new we couldn't really make suggestions about ways to improve participation.

Given the general directive to delegate responsibility, a number of supervisors understood the participative style to mean majority rule. Consequently, they felt their capacity to exercise authority was hampered and they had trouble achieving a workable balance between leadership and participation. One supervisor said:

> The trouble was that everybody got the idea that every decision had to be made by everybody. Then, someone would say, "Why don't you, the supervisor, make the decision—don't ask everybody." Others would say, "Why didn't you ask me?" There has to be a balance.

Some supervisors had a particularly difficult time evaluating the performance of the members of their teams—especially when negative feedback was called for. This was one task not allocated to team members. One supervisor said that he thought participative management and team organization meant that he had to treat everyone alike. Openness and communication seemed incompatible with criticism. Because of such ambiguities, Centerton employees began to question the general effectiveness of team methods.

Another source of frustration was the managers' failure to fulfill employees' requests or adopt their suggestions. The production managers, for example, would ask the supervisors to solicit team suggestions about the equipment required to carry out additional tasks. After the supervisors relayed the teams' suggestions, however, most would be disallowed—sometimes because they involved excessive expense, sometimes because there was no time for acquisition, and sometimes because of simple fiat. After a number of such incidents, subordinates began to view managerial requests for ideas as meaningless. They maintained the belief that, in participative management, suggestions from the team would be accepted; rejection represented a subversion of the basic philosophy.

The level of consulting activity dropped significantly during this troubled period. In comparison with the initial, intensive educational campaign, the consultants made only intermittent efforts to help the organization put into practice the abstract concepts inculcated in training. One production supervisor said: "Before we started up it was a high pressure thing. Since we've been in operation . . . the influence of [the consultants] was very minimal."

Perhaps one of the most important reasons for the decline was the May departure of the Principal Investigator and the assumption of his role by the Participant–Observer. She had joined the consulting team on a part-time basis in November 1973; after the Principal Investigator's departure, she assumed increased responsibility. However, no announcement of the transfer of responsibility was ever clearly made and this resulted in considerable ambiguity about her legitimacy as an active consultant. The Principal Investigator had established a deep rooted, personal credibility; it would have been difficult for anyone to match his charisma. One manager observed:

> [The Participant–Observer] was working very hard, but she was inexperienced. She suffered in comparison with [the Principal Investigator], whom she replaced. It was not a lack of willingness. [The Project Director] also did not have the same personality, the same rapport, that [the Participative Investigator] had.

The Participant–Observer worked primarily on a one-to-one basis, facilitating communication between individuals who were in conflict and providing consultation to managers and supervisors who requested help. In reality, most of the Centerton employees were unaware of the Participant–Observer's position in the plant. Even the supervisors, who had considerably more contact with her than the operators, did not understand her role. As one of the supervisors said: "I didn't realize what her actual function was, nor that we could utilize her as an actual consultant. . . . I thought for the longest period of time that she was here as an observer." To add to the confusion, the relationship between the consulting and research teams was widely misunderstood at the plant. In response to these ambiguities, a fact sheet explaining the roles of each group was issued during the training session for new supervisors held in August 1974. The following month, a statement of Quality of Work Life goals was distributed to all employees.

Differences in work demands and managerial styles between the Production and Quality Assurance departments were reflected in their differential responses to the Participant–Observer. Given its already lengthy list of priorities, the Production Department found it difficult to respond enthusiastically to her suggestions for regular team meetings. In contrast, the Quality Assurance Department regularly held team meetings to air concerns and discuss matters of policy.

Another major difference between the departments involved the use of the questionnaire data collected monthly by the evaluators and later fed back to each Centerton department. In Quality Assurance, the data were posted and used to generate discussion in team and department meetings. Production, in contrast, made limited use of these data. In October 1974 the Participant–Observer began posting survey data on bulletin boards located in departmental work areas. In the Production and Maintenance and Engineering departments, however, the data posted were frequently outdated and stirred little, if any, interest among the employees. It later became clear that the responsibility for keeping the centers up-to-date had never been clarified; thus, neither the Participant–Observer nor the supervisors took over the task.

In addition to team meetings and the establishment of information centers, Quality of Work Life activities included attempts to expand the arenas of team responsibility. For example, team input into personnel policy decisions (e.g., advancement procedures) was sought. In Production, a number of teams participated in team recruitment and selection of new employees. Training programs on Quality of Work Life concepts were periodically held for new hires and supervisors during this period.

In spite of these activities, a fundamental lack of understanding about the goals of the Quality of Work Life program persisted. Perhaps this was not surprising, since neither specific intervention objectives nor a plan for implementation had ever been formally agreed upon by the consultants and Centerton management. A report prepared by the Participant–Observer in April 1975 stated:

> While there are a few partial statements of Centerton's Quality of Work Life goals, there is no precise readily available statement of the goals or plans for implementation. As might be expected, therefore, I find little common understanding of the QWL goals or the project among plant personnel.

Although each party had agreed in principle to implement the project, no detailed design for the change effort had been articulated.

The optimism and zeal that characterized this period gave way to anxiety and self-examination. Both Centerton personnel and the consultants felt uneasy. Problems that had begun to emerge in the early months were, if anything, increasing in magnitude. The Plant Manager remarked:

> We have a most capable group—why aren't we in control? . . . Plant-wide we are not making this happen . . . so many dedicated people can work so long and hard and have so little happen. Is it worth the effort? Is it the plant start-up, Crown Medical headquarters, the lack of engineering, or the lack of people?

The process of self-examination was capped by the staff "Kiem-Tau" session held in November 1974. These sessions, patterned on the "after action" debriefings and group discussions held by the North Vietnamese Army, had been proposed by the consultants as a means of critical self-evaluation. The November meeting was designed to assess Centerton's progress, take note of barriers, and make plans for the future.

This meeting had historic implications for the Quality of Work Life program. Not only did the Plant Manager make it clear that Centerton was engaged in a battle for survival, but the espoused management style was perceived as a barrier to effectiveness and productivity. In particular, it was seen as a major cause of the supervisors' confusion about their roles and authority. The Plant Manager's statement on participative management during the Kiem-Tau was highly significant:

> Participative management, autonomous work groups, or team management looked great but the application is causing problems. Some have come up to me saying, "I feel restrained. I know what to do but my manner of doing it may not live up to this philosophy of management." Generally speaking, I subscribe to this philosophy, but it is more important to feel comfortable with it.
>
> We're not here to sell it. We won't worry about what to call it, be it the Smith style or the Jones style. Think rather about what works for you. Take the objectives only as they improve your ability to do an effective job . . . . There is no substitute for getting the job done. The first priority is to find something that works for you. Don't worry about what to call it, as long as it gives you the confidence and success to work from, an anchor or baseline to give you momentum. Take what you want and what is effective, and put the rest down.

The Plant Manager added that although he subscribed to the Quality of Work Life program, it was no substitute for a successful start-up. At that point in plant development, he noted, the crucial task was to establish a baseline of achievement.

After establishing a baseline, each manager could experiment and develop his or her own style of participative management.

The Plant Manager's address marked a turning point. Many employees saw it as releasing them from strict adherence to the participative philosophy, as signaling a new freedom to adopt a management style based on individual preference, and as elevating production goals above all other considerations. Later describing the significance of the event, the Production Manager said:

> Our priorities have changed and now we're concerned about surviving . . . . Right now productivity is the thing. Participative management has been shelved . . . . There's been a change in my approach. I was spooked by the whole theory of [participative management]. I thought I had to have everyone's wholehearted involvement . . . . With all due respect to [the consultants], everything they said was right, but the priorities are wrong.

Along the same vein, one supervisor said:

> There's no two ways around it. It's blatantly obvious that the supervisors and managers have been given the O.K. to adapt the program to whatever they're comfortable with. As such, the upgrading of the quality of work life in different departments has come to a virtual standstill . . . .

The November Kiem-Tau marked the end of Centerton's participative utopia.

Chapter Five

Centerton Moves Toward Equilibrium

After the Kiem-Tau, numerous important changes took place at Centerton. Although these developments may appear to be radical departures from the utopian days, their origins can be traced to forces that were present in the plant's early history.

To comply with the new focus on productivity, the Plant Manager reorganized Centerton during the few months of late 1974 and early 1975. Personnel changes were accompanied by actions designed to boost production. Scrutiny by Crown management was intensified as Centerton strove to achieve goals set by corporate headquarters. Even as these efforts were underway, however, new crises arose. The new Filtration Manager's blunt, aggressive style created a great deal of dissension among his subordinates. Conflicts between the Plant Manager and the Quality Assurance Manager, long latent, erupted more frequently and openly. Attempts to stimulate production gains were thwarted by frustrating technical bugs in the filtration process.

Eventually, Centerton began to make headway. By the summer of 1975, four products had been licensed, and the plant appeared to be operating at a reasonably steady rate. It was widely believed that this level of development had been achieved through a single-minded pursuit of production objectives. In this atmosphere, the Quality of Work Life project found Centerton an increasingly inhospitable home. The intervention was officially terminated in June 1975, although some contact with the Principal Director continued throughout the year.

The events of this complex period in Centerton's history are detailed in the sections that follow. Key milestones are summarized in a brief chronology of Centerton's early history (Table 5-1).

Table 5-1   Critical Events in the History of Centerton

Date	Centerton	Consultants
1972		
September	Site announced for Centerton plant (9/23)	
1973		
January	Centerton Personnel Manager hired	
	Meeting at corporate headquarters for project planning: Department of Labor, ISR, Consultants (1/30)	
February	Memo of understanding regarding the project (2/21)	
May–June	Centerton/Consultants' planning for training and staffing	
August	Consultants'/Centerton top management interviews of supervisory applications	
September	Ground breaking at Centerton (9/9)	
	Corporate approval of memo of understanding (9/23)	
October		Consultants' management training workshop (10/1–3)
		Managerial and supervisory workshop on QWL (10/24–26)
November		Participant–Observer joins consulting team on a part-time basis

Table 5-1   (Continued)

Date	Centerton	Consultants
		Production and Quality Assurance managers' and supervisors' technical training in Baytown; initial supervisor challenge of commitment to participation
December		Workshop on individual interviewing and employee selection techniques (12/18–21)
1974 January		Initial recruitment and interviewing for production operators (1/7–11)
February	Purchase of Crown Medical Specialties by European firm	New employee training program (2/25)
March		New employee training program (3/3–6)
		Initial production start day
April	Tension among Production Manager and two department managers	Counseling interviews
May		Participant–Observer starts on site full time (5/16)
		Project Director's visit; Principal Investigator leaves for Russia (5/29)
June	Actual plant start-up (first pool) (6/24)	Team discussion of personnel policies
		Team recruitment and selection started
July		Training program for new hires and supervisors (7/10–11)
		Project Director's visit (7/29); personal counseling for managers and supervisors

Table 5-1 (Continued)

Date	Centerton	Consultants
August	First filling operation; delays in filtration	Orientation for new employees (8/19–21) Training for new supervisors Consultants' fact sheet issued (8/23)
September	Staff meeting to examine team organizational style (9/17) First dissolving (9/24) Cost cutting measures; freeze on hiring and wage increases (9/25)	Project Director's visit Training session and individual feedback Summary of consultant and Quality of Work Life roles issued (9/3–4) New supervisor training (9/20)
October	Plasma lots submitted for testing (10/15) First finishing operation (10/28)	New supervisor's training (10/7–8) Participant–Observer sets up information centers for ISR Short Form feedback (10/9) New supervisors' training (10/22)
November	Freeze on hiring First product, plasma protein fraction licensed by Bureau of Biogenics	Participant–Observer meets with supervisors on advancement procedures (11/11) Project Director's visit Consultants' Progress Report for June–December 1974 (restatement of project goals) (11/21)
December	Albumin lots submitted for testing (12/2) Turnover of supervisors (12/16) Transfer of Filtration Manager (12/23)	

Table 5-1   (Continued)

Date	Centerton	Consultants
1975 January	Heavy corporate pressure for profit in early 1975 Reorganization of the Production Department; tightening of controls New Filtration Manager hired Albumin normal serum licensed (1/13) Pooling team created (1/14) Corporate president visits for job analysis and cost cutting Problems between the Quality Assurance Manager and Plant Manager Reorganization of Maintenance Department	New employee training (1/19–21); participation deemphasized Participant–Observer linked with termination decisions and loses credibility Participant–Observer disseminates summary of ISR feedback (1/21) Decline in Quality of Work Life activities and influence
February	Plant Manager starts team representative communication meetings (2/27) Bureau of Biologics grants Centerton a license to produce second product Filtration Department shut down due to production problem Problems with the Filtration Manager's management style	Staff meets and redefines consultant role as "on call" Participative management and job enrichment "placed on hold" (2/14)
March		Visit by Project Director and return of Principal Investigator for communication meeting (3/3–5) New employees' training (3/12–13) Staff meets to discuss Par-

Table 5-1   (Continued)

Date	Centerton	Consultants
		ticipant–Observer's role (3/18)
April	Third product, immune serum globulin, licensed (4/15)	Participant–Observer's report to managers on Quality of Work Life; intervention goals stated explicitly for first time (4/18)
		Project Director's visit to clarify consultants' role; held filtration meeting (4/29–30)
		Decline in Personnel Manager's role in Quality of Work Life
May	Third product licensed by Bureau of Biologics	
	Two-week layoff announced	
	Corporate headquarters opposes participative style due to need for control in the plasma-production process	
	Resumption of supervisor training (5/26)	
June	Consultants meet with supervisors and managers to evaluate project (6/16–18)	
		Official termination of Participant–Observer's presence in Centerton
July	Fourth product licensed	Meeting with corporate management to discuss project (7/28)
	Company wide layoff (7/7–21)	
	Tetanus immune and immune serum globulin licensed (7/8)	
	New fractionation supervisors hired (7/8)	
August	Three new supervisors for Anti-hemophiliac factor (AHF) hired	

Table 5-1 (Continued)

Date	Centerton	Consultants
September	Four managers and supervisors turn over	Supervisor training (9/3,4,6,9,11, and 18)
		Project Director visits (9/3–4)
October		Consultants discuss draft of consultants' report with Centerton employees (10/22–23)
December		
1976		
March	AHF lots submitted for testing (3/30)	
May	AHF licensed (5/30)	

LEADERSHIP PROBLEMS AND REORGANIZATION

Even during the earliest days, when belief in the promise of utopia was strongest, incipient leadership conflicts were apparent at Centerton. A central ingredient was the antagonistic relationship between the Production Manager and his subordinate, the Fractionation Manager. Both men came from the Crown plant at Baytown, where substantial interpersonal friction had developed between them. The decision to move them together to Centerton was considered a calculated risk; however, because of the shortage of technically proficient staff willing to join the new plant, it was a chance Crown management and the consultants were willing to take.

Centerton's difficult start-up days provided ample fuel for ill feeling between the two men. Some of their problems apparently resulted from differences in personal style. The Production Manager was inclined toward a traditional, somewhat authoritarian management style, and tended to treat his co-workers with formality. The Fractionation Manager, on the other hand, was young, brash, and aggressive. A sociable individual, he was friendly with many of his fellow employees. Apart from these differences, the two had conflicting views about the Fractionation Manager's performance. The Production Manager felt that his subordinate had a "can't do" attitude, that he blamed the problems of his department on external factors—for example, imperfect equipment or inadequate maintenance—when some of the department's failings were clearly his own fault. The Production Manager specifically charged that the Fractionation Manager lacked follow-through, and that his frequent angry outbursts alienated others. On the other hand, the Fractionation Manager was frustrated and angry because he felt that the Production Manager failed to provide help when requested.

The problems of the two men influenced the operation of the whole plant, since together they formed the technical base of Centerton's Production Department. Early on, the Project Director devoted a significant portion of his energies to providing counseling and conflict resolution consultation for them. But hostilities continued to grow. After the Project Director left for the Soviet Union in May 1974, the Participant–Observer tried to improve relations between the two managers. She encouraged them to speak more frequently, believing that their avoidance of frank discussion was a central problem that eventually contributed to production performance difficulties. This consultation, however, produced little or no improvement. In their report at the end of 1974, the consultants wrote:

> Much time, effort and counsel was put into aiding the development of this management group. Substantial gain was made in the interpersonal relationship between two of the managers, but little progress was achieved in bringing about effective managerial performance. The most damaging factors in the failure to improve the situation were, first, the managers' tendency to avoid or put off frank discussion of the problem, fol-

lowed by timely performance feedback; and second (when feedback was given), the lack of specific definition of performance deficits and of concrete agreed-upon steps for change.

The continued deterioration of this relationship gradually divided the entire plant as employees took sides. The Plant Manager came to agree with the Production Manager's assessment of the situation and grew increasingly incensed at what he perceived to be the Fractionation Manager's underhanded politicking.

In December 1974 the Plant Manager instituted radical changes in the Production Department. The Fractionation Manager was terminated. The Production Manager's position was eliminated, and the Production Manager took over as Fractionation Manager. Furthermore, the Filtration Manager was moved to a nonmanagerial, staff role in engineering and was replaced by a man with extensive experience in pharmaceuticals.

The termination of the Fractionation Manager was a traumatic milestone. Several months later, the Plant Manager reflected:

> There was no way to get the ship into port with what I had. So I broke the family circle. That shook the foundation of the family, if you will. They're still trying to recover. Every time somebody leaves, either by design or on their own, it shakes the family.

These changes were especially painful for the Production Manager, who was not consulted prior to the changes in his department. Moreover, the move represented a demotion to a position with less responsibility than the one he had held at Baytown. The demotion was especially disappointing because he had moved to Centerton only for the opportunity to step up and in the process had given up a comfortable life in Baytown. His wife's dissatisfaction with the rural Centerton life-style further contributed to his problems. Nevertheless, he agreed wholeheartedly that the termination of the Fractionation Manager was appropriate. He said:

It was a very wise decision but it should have happened a long time ago. It was kind of amazing that he could have so much effect on other key people. And some of these were people he did not like or respect, but he was able to gain their confidence and win influence.

The decision further consolidated the factions that had formed on both sides of the issue. Some supervisors felt that the Fractionation Manager had not been given sufficient warning that his performance was unsatisfactory. Others thought that his termination was unjustified, feeling that he was the victim of his superior's inability to provide guidance. They thought the wrong person had been terminated, and the decision created feelings of insecurity in the ranks. As one supervisor put it: "If this was the way [Fractionation Manager's name], who dedicated his whole life to Centerton, was treated, what chance was there for us?"

The Quality Assurance Manager took the side of the supervisors against the Plant Manager and the Production Manager. Earlier, he had expressed the view that the Plant Manager's pressure for increased production created dangerous risks of contamination and product loss. Like some of the supervisors, he thought that the deficits in production were attributed to employee shortcomings when they should have been blamed on unreliable equipment and inadequate technical help from corporate headquarters. Because the Quality Assurance Manager was widely respected in the plant as a competent and considerate manager, his views carried weight. The Plant Manager later said:

> There was a period of time after the [Fractionation Manager] situation when the plant really chose sides. It was me and [the Production Manager], and it was everybody else and [the Quality Assurance Manager]. No question, it split the plant—not down the middle—down one side.

Although less controversial, the changes made in the Filtration Department were also significant. The Filtration Manager was technically proficient but had no previous managerial experience. He seemed unable to cope with the complicated administrative parts of his job. Thus, the Filtration Department was moving even more slowly than Fractionation.

A new Filtration Manager was hired, in his own words, to be a "clean-up man." He had many years of managerial and pharmaceutical experience. His selection clearly reflected a growing realization within Centerton's managerial ranks that the earlier emphasis on youth and potential had to change. An energetic, hard driving individual, the new manager had a proven ability to get things done. On his office wall hung a sign: "The fellow who says it can't be done is often interrupted by the fellow doing it." In contrast to his predecessor, who tended to procrastinate while reflecting on alternatives, the new manager liked to confront problems directly—even if it meant conflict. He said:

> There are tough decisions to be made and I have the guts to make them. I'm not running a popularity contest . . . matters have to be decided on fact, not emotion. . . . There is a difference between being liked and being respected.

High on his list of "tough decisions" was identifying and eliminating those employees he felt were "dragging their heels." He believed that the Quality of Work Life project had made people too soft and too close. As he put it: "I believe in aggressive people. . . . People were looking for excuses, with no motivation, when I came in. Supervisors were managing people with hearts instead of minds."

Consistent with this philosophy, he told one supervisor: "I didn't know you were a whipped dog like the others." This supervisor later said:

> I saw a tremendous amount of conflict with [the new Filtration Manager] and was ready to run from the fight before it started. I was anticipating problems, listening to other people. . . . If he told me the sun rose at 6:00 AM, I would have said 6:01 AM.

The new Filtration Manager had no tolerance for either the Quality of Work Life project or the consultants. Although he basically agreed with many of the intervention's principles, which he characterized as simply "sound management," he disagreed with the way the intervention was being implemented. He felt that the consultants had raised unattainable expectations. He said: "Sitting out here in Centerton trying to make a utopia just doesn't make sense." He also disparaged the notion of job enrichment by cross-training, at least during a start-up period:

> Job enrichment—having everybody cross-trained on all jobs— is an idealistic concept. You have people that don't want to do it. In a plant start-up we can't have a lot of people (75 percent) half-assed trained in all jobs. Some people must be able to do their jobs 100 percent.

In fact, he made it a point to emphasize his differences with the Centerton "old guard." He said:

> You know I am not a Centerton man. I am not like them. I have no commitment to [the consultants] or to ISR. . . . I feel you have to get the product out first and worry about other things later. You can't put the cart before the horse.

CONSOLIDATION AND CONTINUING CONFLICT

With his revamped management team, the Plant Manager began a new attack on Centerton's production problems. Under increasing pressure from corporate headquarters to show a profit during the first six months of 1975, his first move was to tighten plant controls. He reorganized the Maintenance Department and temporarily assumed personal responsibility for overseeing maintenance operations—much to the dismay of many employees. Expenditures came under even closer scrutiny, and a personnel audit was undertaken to find potential areas for cutbacks. At the same time, he increased the number of people who reported to him directly.

The Plant Manager also instituted employee "communications meetings" to provide him with a direct source of information about lower level operations. Once a month he met with representatives from each team to discuss problems and exchange information. These meetings were seen as a way to foster better understanding among departments, to provide a forum for suggestions, and to exert direct control over operations.

Important production successes followed. In February, the Bureau of Biologics granted Centerton a license to produce a second product; in the spring, approval for a third product was obtained. Fractionation was operating at production design capacity and a new method significantly improved pooling product yield. New finishing and pooling teams were established with remarkably few snags.

But problems continued to trouble Centerton. To many, the Plant Manager's efforts to take charge made him appear dominating and overwhelming. Even the managers installed in corporate headquarters by the new owners wondered how the Quality of Work Life effort could work when the Plant Manager was so authoritarian and directive. Further, some Centerton employees felt that the Plant Manager made all the actual decisions, despite a show of participation. In the words of one, he was "an autocrat behind the facade of open mindedness."

The Plant Manager was aware of some of this resistance to his leadership. According to him: "There was a lot of standing back and saying 'Let's see what he can do with this.' There was some feeling that we started the plant not because we were ready but because I wanted it started."

The Plant Manager felt that he had to be a positive force during this time, a source of energy for Centerton employees. And, although he was aware of the risks involved in changing his managerial style, he also believed that a confident, "take charge" attitude was essential to get the plant moving. He said:

> They [the staff] did not have great experience—therefore they needed certainty in every little step before they could do it—and so I had to generate enough confidence that we were really ready to move, until I came across kind of . . . artificial. They couldn't understand how I could be so positive and so confident that we were ready.

The Plant Manager's leadership problems were exacerbated by his continuing struggle with the Quality Assurance Manager. The split, which had crystallized over the termination of the Fractionation Manager, grew wider as the Quality Assurance Manager and the Plant Manager found more areas of philosophical and operational disagreement.

One of the major issues revolved around a Quality Assurance concern that the Production Department, which was now led by the Plant Manager, had too much control over information and decisions. A serious dispute arose when corporate headquarters moved to have the entire Centerton plant report to the Plant Manager. This was totally unacceptable to the Quality Assurance Manager who believed that separation of Quality Assurance and Manufacturing was a sacred principle. Standards were another concern; the Quality Assurance Manager feared that the Plant Manager was endangering product sterility by succumbing to intense pressure to increase production. The Plant Manager's decision to form a specialized pooling team in the Fractionation Department created still more tension. This action, ostensibly an effort to streamline operations, was interpreted by the Quality Assurance Manager as "throwing job enrichment out the window."

To some extent, the Plant Manager blamed his authority and leadership problems on the consultants. He thought that they provided a "court of appeals" for those who were dissatisfied with his decisions. In his own words:

> People give token support to a decision knowing that in a few weeks they can talk to [the Project Director] or [the Crown Medical Vice President]. I'm not sure it's to the benefit of the plant or myself to have a person come in so people can appeal. They've got to accept me and me them. I'm not sure that having a consultant is facilitating our getting the work done . . .

New production problems compounded his leadership difficulties. Just as the fractionation process began to get ironed out, enormous difficulties emerged in filtration. For the first two months of 1975, the Filtration Department was shut down because of intransigent technical problems. In February, the Production Manager said:

> We have a major crisis at present. We take new plasma and two-thirds of the way through the process, we hit a brick wall—sterility problems in filtration. Production is not going out the door fast enough to cover expenses. . . . The problem is jeopardizing even those who are doing an outstanding job. We're not talking about it because it might "spook the troops."

An interdepartmental task force was formed to attend to the contamination problems in filtration and two technical experts were brought in from corporate headquarters.

In this situation, technological and personnel difficulties once again converged to produce a crisis. Equipment failures occurred while increasing complications arose from the department's managerial transition. The supervisors were appalled at the new Filtration Manager's directive, nonparticipative style. One supervisor likened him to a Marine drill sergeant—he would order things to "get moving" without, the supervisor felt, adequately considering the complexities of the situation. The supervisors wanted him to alter his style, to acknowledge that he knew less about plasma technology than they did. On the other hand, the new Filtration Manager was confounded by their preoccupation with management style, which he considered excessive, and astounded by their lack of attention to performance.

Turnover of key staff created additional problems in the Production Department. Two valuable fractionation supervisors resigned, and many other supervisors began to circulate their resumes in hopes of finding new positions. The physical and mental fatigue stemming from the start-up and the reorganization deepened as rumors circulated from corporate headquarters that Centerton's future was in jeopardy. Employee morale dipped even further with a May announcement that there would be a 2-week layoff in July for all Crown Medical personnel. Corporate's decision to schedule the layoff was based on a sudden drop in sales. The announcement not only highlighted the financial difficulties confronting the company but also emphasized corporate management's assumption that the company's fiscal problems could be addressed, at least partially, by savings in personnel costs. Many Centerton managers disagreed. One said:

> The savings from a two-week layoff will amount to $600,000 in salaries companywide. This represents just over one lot of plasma—they've already lost two lots in the rush trying to get things done.

The layoff announcement was particularly demoralizing because it came shortly after reports from the Crown marketing department that the company was booming and that production could barely keep up with sales. One Centerton employee said:

> In January they told us to tighten our belts and work like hell and that everything would work out. At the end of May, the

sales people came in and said we made their job so easy and things were going great. Two weeks later, Baytown corporate said, "There will be a two-week layoff without pay. We've got millions of dollars worth in the warehouse that we can't sell." What happened?

THE DECLINE OF QUALITY OF WORK LIFE ACTIVITIES

Already debilitated by the deliberate shift away from the Quality of Work Life principles announced at the November Kiem-Tau, the intervention was further weakened by the reorganization of and terminations in the Production Department. Rumors that the Participant–Observer had been involved in the decision to "break up the family" severely undermined her credibility. Many of the supervisors and managers felt that she had become too closely associated with the Plant Manager, and they became increasingly wary of her. One of the supervisors said: "The Participant–Observer has had her chance and it hasn't worked. Most people think she works for [the Plant Manager]."

Changes in the plant's orientation procedures reflected the growing estrangement. In January 1975, the Plant Manager decided to exclude team training workshops from the orientation for new employees, to avoid creating unrealistic expectations about the plant's actual exphasis on team functioning. Instead, individual supervisors were left to determine the degree of adherence to the intervention principles within their teams. During the orientation, the Personnal Manager underscored the boundaries of the participative style of management:

> We want to have a participative company with team effort and team spirit, with high employee morale. This doesn't mean, though, that the team decides everything. . . . Don't mistake it as the employees running the plant.

The Plant Manager's disillusionment with the intervention was clear in his response to a question about the present state of the project: "It is a terrible, crisis time. I'm trying to run a plant, not to do anything special. There were too many different inputs for start-up. We needed more structure to get started." He also commented on the mismatch between the goals of the intervention and the staff's level of experience:

> I would not use this style of management with this kind of group—perhaps if the group was more seasoned. You cannot start a plant with a committee of inexperienced people. . . . There was much idealism, naiveté, and lack of maturity.

In February, a staff meeting formally redefined the consultant's role to be "on call," officially deferring any further efforts to adhere to the principles of job enrichment and participation. Discarding the broad term "job enrichment," Centerton managers agreed to concentrate on a few points—sharing information with the operators; soliciting the operators' suggestions regarding plant problems; developing a system of measuring performance; and providing performance feedback to the operators. The managers also called for the Project Director, who had just returned from the Soviet Union, to help assess the current situation and redefine objectives.

In response to this request, the Principal Investigator and the Project Director conducted a 3-day workshop in March. The meetings were intended to improve communication among the managers and between the managers and the Participant–Observer. The consultants described their role in the workshop this way:

> It seemed to us that problems lying behind the divisiveness, mistrust, frustration, and friction had the best chance of getting resolved if they were brought to the surface and frankly discussed by the top group. . . . Our role would be the discussion facilitator, catalyst, group process observer, resource person, "referee" and perhaps gadfly if need be.

During the meetings, some of the causes of distrust and friction were aired. The Plant Manager invited the others to state frankly their perceptions of his job performance. After this round, each person around the table received the same treatment. However, many of the Centerton staff felt that openness was limited and that the meetings accomplished little. At this point, most seemed simply to have lost heart.

At the March workshop the Participant–Observer offered to prepare a report summarizing the status of the Quality of Work Life project. After her offer was accepted, she interviewed 45 members of Centerton's staff; her report was released the following month. Although the report contained recommendations for future intervention activities, both the consultants and the Centerton management knew that the Quality of Work Life project was in its final days. They considered the possibility of formally ending the project before the originally scheduled date, but decided to keep to the original plan and terminate the project on June 30. Until then, the Participant–Observer was to be available to managers who wanted her assistance. During the last week of April, the Plant Manager made it clear that the Quality of Work Life project was to keep a low profile. He stipulated that no new demands could be made of the managers and supervisors; initiative was to come only from them, not the consultants. The managers and supervisors were to concentrate on doing their jobs. Management had completely abandoned its early preoccupation with attitudes and feelings and now focused solely on task performance. The Plant Manager said: "People are tired of working on relationships instead of working on the job."

Perceived corporate hostility to the project reinforced management's resolve. Apparently, corporate officers considered the project's foremost concern to be an ill-conceived attempt to make everyone happy. In May, they expressed formal objection to the Quality of Work Life project on the grounds that it fostered a management style incongruent with the control needed for plasma production. Corporate officers also felt that much of the divisiveness at Centerton resulted from inadequate discipline associated with the project's permissiveness. This development dampened the little remaining enthusiasm for the Quality of Work Life intervention.

During the final days of the program, the Project Director raised a number of thoughtful questions about the feasibility and limits of the espoused management style. He wondered: "Can you be too open? Can you leave yourself too vulnerable with this degree of openness?"

And he acknowledged that participative management was not an easy style to adopt:

> Assuming leadership in this kind of atmosphere and making management decisions was not easy. It may have created some sticky problems, and some hard decisions had to be made. Some feelings may have been hurt badly. Maybe we did make a mistake, making this kind of management look easy.

Reflecting on their experiences, Centerton managers and employees posed many of these same questions. The Centerton Quality of Work Life program ended as scheduled, and the Participant–Observer left the plant at the end of June.

QUASI-STATIONARY EQUILIBRIUM

In the period between July 1975 and July 1976, the Centerton plant emerged from its start-up period. Process and equipment problems, while still present, were no longer serious. Plant production increased slowly but steadily. In July 1975, the fourth Centerton product was approved by the Bureau of Biologics. Three supervisors were hired in August to oversee the manufacture of a new product, which was put into production in early 1976 and was licensed in June of the same year.

This period was marked by relative calm and increasing self-assurance. In August 1975, the President of Crown Medical Specialties issued a statement in the corporate newsletter that reflected these feelings:

> Crown Medical has been faced with a number of frustrating problems for a number of years. . . . We have aggressively attacked the problems in the last 15 months and can truthfully say that today we have solved many of our problems. . . . Today, after taking strong action and through diligent effort by many of you, we have finished the first half of 1975 with excellent results.

His optimism seemed justified. By the end of our study, Centerton's start-up turbulence had given way to stability and steady growth.

CENTERTON'S DEVELOPMENTAL STAGES

Table 5-1 documents the critical events in Centerton's developmental history. Although there was some overlap among phases, the plant's beginning conforms quite closely to the theoretical predictions of Chapter 2. Its organizational life began with a "utopian fantasy": a new facility in which the managment style would be participative, jobs challenging, and both individual motivation and organizational productivity high. The consultants worked hard during this period to propagate these ideals, especially among the managers and supervisors, and this core group firmly believed that their ideals could be translated into reality.

Even during this idealistic period, however, the sources of future disillusionment were at work. The combination of new staff and new technology created obstacles that appeared at times to be insurmountable. Malfunctions were all too frequent, causing numerous delays in the start-up schedule. It became increasingly evident that the implementation of espoused Quality of Work Life principles would not be easy, particularly in an atmosphere charged with uncertainty and tension.

By the second half of 1974, it was clear that the utopian bubble had burst. The Kiem-Tau marked the plant's official release from adherence to the principles of the Quality of Work Life program.

Events of the plant's second phase of "leadership challenge" came to a head in December with the termination of the Fractionation Manager, an old-time Crown Medical employee with a large and committed following in the plant. This termination split the plant's loyalties as conflicts continued into January 1975 between the Quality Assurance Manager and the Plant Manager.

Stage III, a period of consolidation and problem resolution, began in early 1975. The termination of the Fractionation Manager was accompanied by other personnel and structural changes. A new Filtration Manager was hired and the Production and Maintenance departments were reorganized. The Plant Manager, responding to intense corporate pressure for production, centralized many functions and tightened controls. He organized a series of "team communication meetings" to establish direct lines to production operations.

This period of relative calm was accompanied by conflicts precipitated by the new Filtration Manager. His brusque and aggressive manner offended his colleagues and subordinates. He was openly scornful of the plant's management style, which he perceived to be soft and prone to conflict avoidance. At the same time, he was disturbed by the scrutiny and disapproval his own style evoked at the plant, particularly because it reinforced his perception that the Centerton focus was on style rather than accomplishment.

This fourth period of interpersonal conflict lessened as internal tensions dissipated and the plant worked its way toward equilibrium. By the end of 1975, Centerton had moved beyond its idealistic hopes and the wrenching growing pains of its earlier days. Both production and personnel problems were manageable, and steady progress could be seen.

In the next major section of the book—Chapters 6 to 8—we describe in detail our assessment of the Centerton Quality of Work Life program. Then, in the final section of the book, we reflect on the Centerton experience and draw implications for the creation of high involvement work settings.

PART THREE

MEASURING THE EFFECTIVENESS OF THE QUALITY OF WORK LIFE PROGRAM

Chapter Six

Methodology

CHARACTERISTICS OF THE RESEARCH

There are a number of good reasons to test social interventions in field settings. In particular, research in the natural environment provides an element of sustained realism that is difficult, if not impossible, to introduce in the laboratory.

At the same time, the difficulties of evaluating a complex field project are formidable. Field research typically lacks the experimental isolation and precise control found in laboratory settings. Laboratory research allows one to specify the independent variable with some certainty, but the causal forces that operate in the natural environment are frequently confounded and difficult to identify.

Our research incorporates a number of features that have been tailored to the special requirements of field research (see Lawler, Nadler, & Cammann, 1980). First, the research project is based on a *third-party model*, also called the "split-role field experiment" (Barnes, 1971). This design, which incorporates independent intervention and evaluation functions, is intended to maximize the opportunity for independent, objective assessment of complex field intervention; for the comparison of diverse perspectives; and for the effective implementation of the

115

often contradictory goals of change and evaluation (Nieva & Perkins, 1980).

Second, the evaluation includes not only an assessment of outcomes, but also an analysis of how those outcomes were reached. This dual focus is essential, since a simple evaluation of "success or failure" does not lead to an understanding of the underlying causal forces. As Suchman (1967) and Weiss (1972) have observed, failure may occur either because a program failed to trigger intended causal processes, or because the causal processes, once set in motion, failed to achieve the anticipated outcomes.

These contingencies give rise to two principal implications. First, it is clear that both a valid theory and a workable intervention are essential for a successful outcome to be achieved. Second, and perhaps more important methodologically, an adequate test of theory must include a determination of the extent to which the intervention program was actually implemented in the field. This determination is needed to avoid the appraisal of "non-events" (Charters & Jones, 1973); that is, to minimize the risk that, in reality, no independent variable existed. To claim that an intervention had failed when in fact it had not been effectively implemented would constitute an abject misrepresentation; it would lead to the erroneous conclusion that the intervention did not lead to anticipated results (Freeman & Sherwood, 1965).

The process analysis was further intended to determine which components of the intervention were effective. Many social interventions consist of multiple changes introduced over an extended period; evolving field contingencies frequently give rise to modifications of consulting strategies. Thus, a detailed "microanalysis" must be undertaken to identify the relationships between particular components of the intervention and observed outcomes.

A third feature of the present research arose from the need to include in the evaluation a broad range of systemic, group, and individual variables. This requirement arose for two reasons. First, the specific variables that the consultants expected to influence were, at the beginning of the research, only vaguely defined. Second, we were sensitive to possible unintended consequences of the intervention; that is, the possibility that the consultants might produce outcomes neither they nor the researchers had anticipated. Thus the assessment relied on qualitative methods—such as open-ended interviews—and a "broadband" survey instrument which incorporated a wide range of variables believed to be important measures of organizational and individual functioning (*Michigan Organizational Assessment Package*, 1975).

A final characteristic of the research framework arose from the realization that field studies are typically characterized by a poor "signal to noise" ratio, and that findings can be distorted by reliance on a single method of data collection. Many polemical discussions in the social science literature have centered around the relative merits of structured, statistically testable techniques, and "richer," clinically oriented methods (Glaser & Strauss, 1967). This antagonism of method is not a necessary one, however. Sieber (1973), for example, has argued that the integration of structured survey methods and unstructured field methods provides the closest approximation to reality. And other theorists (e.g., Webb, Campbell, Schwartz, & Sechrest, 1966; Caparaso & Roos, 1973) have called for more extensive use of multiple operationalism—that is, corroborating the results of one research method with those of another.

This process of "triangulation" minimizes the possibility that research conclusions are simply artifacts of the method of data gathering. As Webb et al. (1966) note:

> Once a proposition has been confirmed by two or more independent measurement processes, the uncertainty of its interpretation is greatly reduced. The most persuasive evidence comes through a triangulation of measurement processes. If a proposition can survive the onslaught of a series of imperfect mea-

sures, with all their irrelevant error, confidence should be placed in it. (p. 31)

When feasible, such a "multiple method" approach was followed in the present research, which included questionnaires, interviews, naturalistic observation, and the analysis of archival data.

DATA COLLECTION METHODS

Questionnaires

Pre-Employment Questionnaire. The first data collection in January 1974 employed a Pre-Employment Questionnaire given to all those who applied for positions in the new organization. This questionnaire, which dealt with issues of job design, supervision, and individual characteristics, was later used to compare the characteristics of those selected and those not selected.

Short Form Questionnaire. The Short Form Questionnaire, an abbreviated version of the core survey instrument (the Michigan Organizational Assessment), was administered monthly from July 1974 to June 1975, and bimonthly from August 1975 to December 1975. The Short Form Questionnaire contained questions dealing with a broad range of research variables, including satisfaction, motivation, organizational climate, likelihood of turnover, decision making, supervision, and pay.

During the months in which the longer Michigan Organizational Assessment was administered, the Short Form items were included in it. Response rates for the Short Form Questionnaire (Table 6-1) varied from department to department and from administration to administration. The decline in

Table 6-1 Response Rates for the Short Form Questionnaire

| | Centerton Unit | | | | | |
| | Quality Assurance | | Production | | Total Plant | |
Month	Number	Percentage	Number	Percentage	Number	Percentage
July 1974	17	74	24	74	60	70
August 1974	16	67	21	58	52	57
September 1974	15	61	18	43	49	50
October 1974	19	76	23	54	58	58
November 1974*	25	100	34	83	80	81
December 1974	22	90	12	29	55	56
January 1975	21	89	17	35	55	50
February 1975	25	100	26	50	77	66
March 1975	24	100	30	59	75	66
April 1975	23	96	23	45	64	52
May 1975	22	94	25	48	64	50
June 1975	20	91	20	40	57	47
August	19	83	24	48	66	55
October 1975	21	91	29	56	75	56
December 1975*	21	93	37	72	98	75

* Short Form administered within Michigan Organizational Assessment questionnaire.

119

response rates is most probably attributable to the later hiring of individuals unacquainted with the Quality of Work Life project; increasing time pressures associated with the plant start-up; and growing disenchantment with the intervention. One department, Quality Assurance, recorded a participation rate which neared 100 percent at most administrations. This enthusiasm appeared to result from the Quality Assurance Manager's encouragement—and benign coercion—and from the knowledge that the survey results would be used in a systematic way to effect organizational changes. The Quality Assurance area was the only department to consistently use questionnaire data in this way.

Michigan Organizational Assessment (MOA). The Time 1 Michigan Organizational Assessment was administered at Centerton in November 1974. Later analyses suggested that some items could be excluded without substantial loss of information, and abbreviated versions were administered at both Centerton and Baytown at Time 2. Finally, data were collected from the Centerton plant in January 1977, the final Time 3 assessment.

Our original research plan included a nonequivalent comparison site, Baytown, which we thought would provide some benchmarks for assessing the impact of the Quality of Work Life programs. As will be discussed later, however, our inability to gain access to T_1 or T_3 data from Baytown, coupled with substantial differences between the two organizations, severely limited the usefulness of the Baytown T_2 survey.

All administrations of the Michigan Organizational Assessment included items from the following standardized modules:

1. *Demographics.* This module contained items addressing background characteristics of individual respondents, such as age, marital status, and ethnic identification.

2. *General Work Attitudes.* This module addressed such employee attitudes as job satisfaction, likelihood of leaving the organization, intrinsic motivation, and performance outcomes.

3. *Job Facets—Importance and Contingencies.* This module assessed a number of aspects of an individual employee's orientation and reaction to his or her job. Included in this section were measures of the perceived importance of various job facets and outcomes, and employee beliefs that especially good or poor performance would lead to an increase or a decrease in the extent to which those facets are present in his or her job.

4. *Task and Role Characteristics.* The purpose of this module was to assess employees' perceptions of the characteristics of the tasks performed as a part of their jobs, and to obtain descriptions of the constraints and pressures placed upon them in their work roles.

5. *Work Group Functioning.* This module assessed work group characteristics, with a primary focus on work group norms, the nature of its members, their behaviors, and the effectiveness of the work group design.

6. *Supervisory Behavior.* This module examined the way in which employees' supervisors are perceived. Descriptions of competence, style, and general leadership behavior were obtained.

7. *Intergroup Relations.* This module assessed the quality of intergroup relationships, including sources of conflict and modes of conflict resolution.

8. *Influence Structure.* This module dealt with the extent to which employees felt they could and should influence decisions made in the operation of the organization.

9. *Individual Differences.* This module assessed employee attitudes about life in general, and such individual characteristics as openness to change, self-esteem, and the extent to which employees felt they had control over meaningful events in their lives.

Specification of each Michigan Organizational Assessment index, component items, and measures of internal consistency (Cronbach alpha) can be found in Nieva, Perkins, and Lawler (1978). Response rates for the Michigan Organizational Assessment administrations at Centerton and Baytown are shown in Table 6-2. The demographic characteristics of participants are included in Table 6-3.

Goal Attainment Survey. In April 1975 the Participant–Observer developed a comprehensive list of the goals the Quality of Work Life program attempted to reach. Following a

Table 6-2   Response Rates for the Michigan Assessment of Organizations

Administration Date	Centerton		Baytown	
	Number Responding	Percentage of Total Plant	Number Responding	Percentage of Total Plant
November 1974	80	81	—	—
December 1975	98	75	131	64.6
January 1977	119	61	—	—

Forty-nine individuals responded at both Time 1 and Time 2 Centerton administrations. 50 completed questionnaires at Time 2 and Time 3, and 36 individuals responded to all three Centerton questionnaires.

Table 6-3   Demographic Characteristics of Those
Completing the Michigan Assessment of Organizations at
Centerton

	Administration					
	Time 1		Time 2		Time 3	
Characteristic	N	%	N	%	N	%
Age						
Under 21	7	8.9	7	7.2	8	6.8
21–30	57	72.2	61	62.9	80	67.8
31–40	9	11.4	19	19.6	22	18.6
41–50	5	6.3	8	8.2	6	5.1
51–60	1	1.3	2	2.1	2	1.7
Over 60	0	0.0	0	0.0	0	0.0
Race						
White	72	90.0	84	88.0	97	81.5
Black	7	9.0	9	9.0	22	18.5
Other	1	1.0	3	3.0	0	0.0
Sex						
Male	53	66.0	61	62.0	74	62.7
Female	27	34.0	37	38.0	44	37.3
Education						
Elementary school	0	0.0	1	2.0	0	0.0
High school	22	28.0	32	33.0	33	28.0
College	53	66.0	56	59.0	76	65.0
Beyond college	5	6.0	6	6.0	8	7.0

variant of the goal attainment scaling technique proposed by
Kiresuk and Sherman (1968), these goals (e.g., "openness to
consideration of change," and "when practical, work is done by
small teams") were incorporated into a survey instrument
which measured respondents' perceptions of the extent to
which each was achieved.

In addition, the Goal Attainment Survey dealt with such
issues as the extent of respondents' contact with the consultants, their satisfaction with the consultants, their satisfaction
with the work of the change team, and the conduct of the
Institute for Social Research evaluation team.

Because these issues were extraordinarily complex, it was decided to combine questionnaire and open-ended interview formats in this phase of the research. It was felt that this "internaire" format would enable the research group to gain deeper understanding of the participants' reaction to the experiment and, at the same time, permit standardized comparison of their responses. Although infrequently used, such a format has been recommended by other researchers; for example, Porter and Steers (1973) write:

> With a few notable exceptions, the "limited alternative" questionnaire technique has been used almost exclusively in the attitudinal research on withdrawal. The singular use of such a procedure, while advantageous for statistical and analytical purpose, may have the effect of omitting from consideration important areas relevant to an individual's withdrawal decision. In this regard, it appears that a useful strategy would be the increased use of supplemental data collection techniques (e.g., open-ended interviews) in concert with questionnaires. (p. 170)

At the conclusion of the intervention, such "internaire" discussions were held with all those who had actively participated in the Quality of Work Life program and were willing to share their perceptions with the research team. In all, 85 employees met with the researchers to discuss the intervention; 78 later completed the Goal Attainment Survey.

Exit Questionnaire. Each employee who left the Centerton plant was asked to complete the Exit Questionnaire, a standardized survey about the Centerton work environment. In addition to asking about the importance of some 48 job characteristics in the employees' decisions to leave, the Exit Questionnaire included a series of open-ended questions dealing with turnover issues. Of the 45 employees who left Centerton during the assessment period, 30 completed the Exit Questionnaire.

Questionnaire Administration. Procedures for data collection were tailored to the characteristics and objectives of each instrument. Pre-Employment Questionnaires were handed to each job applicant by a member of the research team. Short Form Questionnaires were distributed in sealed envelopes by departmental secretaries, then deposited in one of three locked boxes—to which only Institute for Social Research evaluators held keys. Exit Questionnaires were mailed to employees who left the organization—a procedure which initially met with little success. To deal with the problem of no returns, a $5.00 incentive was offered for completing the questionnaire. This procedure made a dramatic difference, and very few refused to respond after it had been initiated.

The longer questionnaires were administered by Institute for Social Research researchers who generally met with teams, or small groups of employees, to explain the purpose of the research and to answer questions about the evaluation. These meetings were held in locations adjacent to employees' work areas—for example, in the team meeting rooms for production staff, and in the department conference room for members of the Quality Assurance Department.

The Goal Attainment Survey was administered in much the same way, except that group discussions of the Quality of Work Life program were held after the questionnaires had been completed. These discussions typically began with employees' reactions to the survey instrument, and continued with elaborations on participants' responses. Depending on the nature of the group, these preliminary remarks expanded to include such topics as the effectiveness of consultant techniques; the future of the Quality of Work Life program; expectations about the use of evaluation results; and internal organizational politics. They provided, therefore, a unique opportunity to gather evaluative information in open-ended dialogues with those participating in the Centerton Quality of Work Life project.

Naturalistic Observation

In January 1974, two site historians began visiting the Centerton plant to document the nature of the consultants' interventions, observe the daily functioning of the organization, speak with key individuals about the progress of the Quality of Work Life project, and perform a limited number of administrative tasks—such as gathering personnel data and collecting questionnaires. Although the frequency of site visits varied over the course of the intervention, observations lasting from one to three days were generally made at 2-week intervals.

This commitment to firsthand observation of the change effort was made in the belief that a simple "input–output" analysis of the project's implementation would be an inadequate basis for interpreting the causal forces underlying observed outcomes. As Guttentag and Struening (1975) have noted, the precise nature of the independent variables subsumed by a social intervention is frequently difficult to specify. It may be more accurately represented as a variegated "set" of interventions. For example, a change agent whose activities are officially based on principles of process consultation may also provide expert advice on job design or may assist in personal growth counseling. Thus the need to specify the nature of the consulting intervention, and the difficulty in gathering this information with more structured methods, made frequent on-site observation a practical necessity.

In addition to this function, unstructured observation served two other purposes. First, an attempt was made to gather observational data on variables already assessed through questionnaires and interviews. These observations were useful as a means of assessing the reliability and validity of findings and directing analysis in the event of discrepancies between methods. Second, this clinical approach to evaluation assisted the researchers in taking a holistic view, permitting the program to be analyzed "as a dynamic, complexly interrelated entity" (Glaser & Backer, 1972, p. 54). Thus firsthand observation of the intervention was employed to prevent a fragmented analysis of the qualitative data; structured quantitative approaches were used to provide a check against the biases which could arise through the exclusive application of clinical methods. In a sense, our observation put meat on the bare bones of the statistical reports, and our quantitative data provided a metric for calibrating the results of the project.

Although the naturalistic observation was purposely designed to function in an unstructured way, systematic records of the site historian's observations were maintained. Observer recording forms (see Figure 6-1) were used to provide a running record of events, and a serious attempt was made to separate "objective" description from the site historian's personal reactions. These subjective responses, although a rich source of data in themselves (Glaser & Strauss, 1967), were used to identify potential sources of bias and distortion, providing another means of interpreting the data collected through clinical observation. Finally, the recording form was designed to permit coding of variables and behavior categories; this facilitated the integration of data collected over the two years of site historian visits.

Interviews

Although formal interviews were the least frequently employed method of data collection, interviews were used on a number of occasions. In some instances, for example, a formal interview represented the most straightforward means of obtaining data from key informants known to possess firsthand information about the Quality of Work Life program. In other cases, respondents held organizational roles that allowed them a unique overview of organizational functioning, and semi-structured interviews with these individuals (see Figure 6-2)

	SITE HISTORIAN REPORT		
OBSERVER:		DATE: SITE:	
TIME	DESCRIPTION OF EVENT	WORKING HYPOTHESIS/ COMMENT	VARIABLE CODE

Figure 6-1   Observer recording forms.

INTERVIEW GUIDE

1. Can you tell me something about your job:
   a. What is your role in the organization?
   b. How do you spend your time?
   c. Who do you come in contact with?
   (Probe: To what extent are the following characteristics present: autonomy, variety, task identity, feedback, stress?)
2. What aspects of your job do you like? Which do you dislike?
   (Probe: How important are various individual needs: existence, relatedness, growth? How satisfied is the respondent?)
3. Can you tell me something about your relationship with other teams? Other departments?
   (Probe: What is the quality of working relationship?)
4. Please tell me something about your supervisor:
   a. What does he or she do?
   b. How satisfied are you with his or her performance?
5. How is power distributed in the organization? Who has "say" over what? (Probe: Try to construct a control graph of the organizational influence structure.)
6. How would you describe the organizational climate at Centerton? What does it feel like to work here?
7. How is conflict resolved?
   a. In your team?
   b. In your department?
   c. Throughout the organization?
   (Probe: Do employees rely on confrontation smoothing, fate mechanisms, compromise, or third parties?)
8. How much contact have you had with the consultants (mention names)? What kinds of consultants' activities were you involved in?
   (Probe: Did you find them helpful? How?)
9. How important are influences outside the organization (e.g., corporate headquarters)?
10. Are there other things we should know to understand Centerton? To understand the work of the consultants?

Figure 6-2   Semistructured interview guide.

complemented data collected through questionnaires. Finally, it was also found that—as a practical matter—the interview was sometimes a less obtrusive device than informal, unstructured observation. The presence of an observer with no specified task sometimes caused uneasiness among employees who were initially suspicious of the research. The appearance of "lurking" could be eliminated in these situations by scheduling a formal interview, which was a relatively familiar means of data collection. (Each employee had experienced an employment interview as part of the organization's selection and screening procedures.)

The need for the imposition of such structure varied across time and situation. As the observers became more familiar to the organizational members, integration into ongoing plant activities was easier. The site historians, for example, were later able to engage in clinical observation while assisting a plasma processing team in the production process or joining employees for lunch in the cafeteria. In these instances, a site historian became an active participant or, more accurately, an "observer as participant" (Glaser & Backer, 1972; Gold, 1970); consequently, the need for a more formal means of data collection (i.e., interviews) was less acute.

Access to interview data was also facilitated by the desire of many employees to express their frustrations to the evaluators, who held no position in the organizational hierarchy and had no formal ties with the consultants. This was particularly true in later stages of the intervention, when disenchantment grew. As one manager commented: "I can look at ISR and say, 'That is an outside group.' So [I said things] that I would not have said to [the plant manager], and didn't feel comfortable saying to [the consultants]." The close relationship that developed between researchers and employees proved to be both a strength and a weakness of the research, as we will discuss at the conclusion of this chapter.

Archival Data

As Webb et al. (1966) have observed, archival sources represent one of the least reactive means of data collection in the social sciences. Although biases may result from selective deposit or survival of data, institutional records can provide direct information about individual behavior. In the present research, archival data relating to turnover and absenteeism were collected from both Centerton and Baytown sites for the period April 1974 to February 1976. In addition, information on industry turnover rates was obtained from a United States Department of Labor Publication, *Employment and Earning.*

Company records were also used to explore effects of the Quality of Work Life program on productivity. We originally planned to collect productivity data from both Centerton and Baytown and use the comparison as an indicator of the success of the Centerton start-up. Productivity data were collected for a period beginning January 1975 and ending May 1976. However, for reasons to be discussed later, these data proved to be of limited utility in evaluating the effectiveness of the Quality of Work Life program.

RESEARCH DESIGN AND ANALYSIS

It became unmistakably clear that the research approach had to be flexible enough to accommodate unexpected changes in the Quality of Work Life program. In many ways, this study was an "adaptive experiment" (Lawler, 1977): Early research designs and data collection methods were altered, and new strategies were developed as the study evolved.

As the research progressed, for example, it became increasingly clear that a critical evaluation task would consist of integrating the large quantity and variety of data that had been collected. It also became evident that the evolving Quality of Work Life program would have to be evaluated in phases; that is, different data collection and analytical strategies were appropriate for different periods. The strategies eventually adopted in evaluating each phase of the intervention are described below.

The First Stage of the Intervention

Analysis of the first stage of the intervention focused on the effectiveness of the procedures used to select the initial group of operators in the Centerton plant. The data used in this analysis were taken from four sources: the Pre-Employment Questionnaire administered in January 1974; interviews and observations gathered by the two site historians during this period; and the interview ratings obtained for applicants referred to the initial interview.

Outcomes of the selection process were examined by comparing the selected with the rejected applicants on the Pre-Employment Questionnaire and on supervisors' ratings. Planned comparisons of supervisors, those selected, and those not selected were also made. The selection process itself is described in Chapter 5, and our analytical procedures are detailed in Nieva, Perkins, and Lawler (1980).

The Second Stage of the Intervention

Evaluation of the second stage of the intervention was considerably more varied and complex than that of the first. With the exception of the Pre-Employment Questionnaire, analyses of this stage used a combination of all the data collection instruments incorporated in the study.

The conceptual framework for these analyses was guided by the hypothesized model of intervention effects shown in Figure 6-3. On the basis of the model, we expected that the interven-

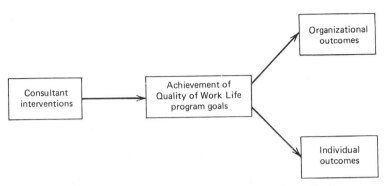

Figure 6-3   Predicted model of intervention effects.

tion techniques of the consultants (e.g., role modeling of participatory behavior) would lead to the accomplishment of goals that had been established for the Quality of Work Life program. We further expected that the attainment of these goals would result in changes in a set of organizational variables (e.g., turnover and productivity), as well as individual outcomes (e.g., job satisfaction and self-esteem).

This framework is somewhat oversimplified. We later found, for example, that certain "outcome" variables actually seemed to produce changes in variables we had labeled as intervening. Nevertheless, the model proved to be a useful means of organizing the evaluation and describing the effects of the Quality of Work Life program at Centerton.

Evaluating the Effectiveness of Consultant Interventions. The evaluation of the effectiveness of consulting methods (see Chapter 7) was based primarily on responses to the Goal Attainment Survey, interviews with employees, and observer records. For the Goal Attainment Survey, employees were asked to indicate the extent to which they were personally affected by the consultants' methods; ratings ranged from one ("This did not affect me at all") to four ("This had a moderate affect on me") to seven ("This affected me a great deal"). Student *t*-tests were used to test the significance of differences between departments on these measures.

Quality of Work Life Goal Achievements at Centerton.
The assessment of Quality of Work Life goal achievement (see Chapter 7), like our evaluation of consultant methods, was based on survey data, interviews, and observation. The responses of Centerton employees to direct questions concerning the extent to which certain specified goals had been achieved at Centerton formed the basis of this evaluation. Again, comparisons between departments were tested for significance using the Student *t*-test.

Effects of the Quality of Work Life Program.
The impact of the program on outcome (O) variables (see Chapter 8) was originally to be based on a Non-Equivalent Control Group Design (Campbell & Stanley, 1963) diagrammed as follows:

$$\frac{O_{C_1} \quad X \quad O_{C_2}}{[O_{B_1}] \quad \quad O_{B_2}}$$

where C = Centerton
     B = Baytown
     X = The Quality of Work Life program

It was intended that the "treatment" group at Centerton would be compared to a nonequivalent comparison group (the Baytown plant), taking into account initial differences between the two organizations. Unfortunately, uncertainties associated with the acquisition of Crown Medical Specialties precluded the Baytown Time 1 measurement $[O_{B_1}]$. Comparisons were limited, therefore, to Time 2 assessments of Centerton and Baytown $[O_{C_2}$ and $O_{B_2}]$.

From these data alone it was impossible to identify the source of observed changes. For example, shifts in the attitudes of Centerton employees could just as plausibly be ascribed to maturational processes as to the Quality of Work Life program. Thus, although comparisons between Baytown and Centerton could suggest program effects, the lack of a pretest measure in Baytown and the lack of similarity between plants severely limited the inferences to be drawn from these data.

Conclusions concerning the effects of the Quality of Work Life program were, therefore, reached by other means. We searched for convergence among multiple data sources: interviews and naturalistic observations, the Goal Attainment Survey, the Exit Questionnaire, monthly attitudinal and behavioral data, and the Michigan Organizational Assessment. In addition, inferences concerning effects of the intervention were drawn (1) from comparisons of Centerton departments that accepted or rejected the intervention; and (2) by the examination of factors that differentiated individuals who interacted with the consultants to a greater or lesser extent. These approaches will be reviewed briefly.

Impact of Departmental Membership. The first approach is, in essence, a Non-Equivalent Control Group Design (Campbell & Stanley, 1963) based on groups internal to the Centerton organization.

The success of the Quality of Work Life program in the Quality Assurance Department, coupled with its rejection by the Production Department (discussed more fully in Chapter 7), provided an opportunity to employ this design, which is diagrammed as follows:

$$\frac{O_{QA_1} \quad X \quad O_{QA_2}}{O_{P_1} \qquad O_{P_2}}$$

where QA = Quality Assurance Department
   P = Production Department
   X = The Quality of Work Life program

Although both units had participated in the Quality of Work Life program until November 1974, the Production Department "shelved" the consultants' ideas in this month—believing that the project was inhibiting production progress. This event coincided with the Time 1 administration of the Michigan

Organizational Assessment; it appeared logical, therefore, to expect that the effects of the Quality of Work Life program might be observed by comparing the development of the two departments subsequent to the November survey.

Statistical procedures for analyzing such developmental differences are controversial (see Cronbach & Furby, 1970; Davidson, 1972; Hummel-Rossi & Weinberg, 1975; Lord, 1967; Tucker, Damarin, & Messik, 1966). No preeminent analytical strategy has emerged from the debate, but Kenny (1975) argues persuasively that—when assignment to treatment and comparison groups is based on preexisting group differences—a standardized change score analysis is least likely to introduce misleading biases. At Centerton, group differences (e.g., greater motivation to participate in the Quality of Work Life program) appeared to be a major factor in the Quality Assurance Department's acceptance of the consultant's ideas. The standardized change analysis thus seemed to be particularly appropriate.

In essence, the standardized change analysis compares (1) the correlation of group membership ("treatment") and a pretest measure with (2) the correlation of group membership ("treatment") and post-test scores. These relationships are shown in Figure 6-4 where the null hypothesis of no treatment effect is simply that $r_{T \cdot X_1} = r_{T \cdot X_2}$. Equality of treatment effect correlations was tested as suggested by McNemar (1969, p. 158) by a formula which accounts for the autocorrelation of pretest and post-test measures $(r_{X_1 \cdot X_2})$.

An example may help to clarify this procedure. To examine the effects of departmental membership on self-esteem, a "dummy" treatment variable (T) was first created by coding Quality Assurance as "one" (representing "treatment") and Production as "zero" (representing "absence of treatment"). Next, the correlation between this variable (T) and self-esteem at Time 1 (X_1) was computed $(r_{T \cdot X_1} = .36)$. The correlation between departmental membership (T) and self-esteem at

Time 1   Time 2

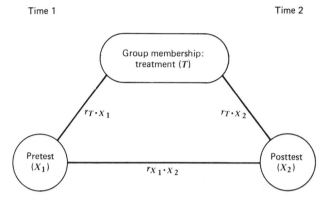

Figure 6-4   Null hypothesis tested by standardized change score analysis.

Time 2 (X_2) was then determined $(r_{T \cdot X_2} = .25)$. Finally, the correlation between Time 1 and Time 2 measures $(r_{X_1 \cdot X_2})$ was found to be .34.

These values were then entered in the formula previously cited, yielding *t*-value of .56, distributed with $N - 3$ degrees of freedom. For the sample tested $(N = 36)$, this value was not statistically significant.

Impact of Interaction with Consultants. In the previously described standardized change analysis, "treatment" was assumed to result from membership in the participative Quality Assurance Department, and "absence of treatment" represented membership in the Production Department—which generally rejected the consultants' concepts. It also seemed possible, however, that the effects of the intervention were transmitted not through departmental membership, but rather through direct interaction between change agents and individual employees.

To explore this possibility, intervention effects were further examined using a procedure proposed by Cook and Campbell

(1975). This method of "treatment effect correlation" represents an extension of the standardized change score analysis proposed by Kenny (1975). It is appropriate when there exist multiple levels of a quantitative measure representing the "take" of an independent variable. For example, Cook and Campbell (1975) suggest that one may be able

> to measure a naturally occurring continuous variable whose effects are to be assessed (e.g., the number of hours worked, the percentage of time spent on the job, etc.) or one will be able to measure the extent to which units in a single treatment group have actually received the intended treatment. (p. 294)

Such a surrogate measure of treatment was available through the Goal Attainment Survey items, for example, "Approximately how much contact did you have with the consultants?" One item was included for each of the three consultants, and responses were measured on a 7-point scale ranging from one ("Never") to seven ("Once a day"). These three items were averaged to form an index of consultant contact, which was then correlated with both pretest and post-test measures. The null hypothesis of no treatment was then tested as in the conventional standardized change score analysis.

Causal Relationships

Causal forces within Centerton were explored using the method of cross-lagged panel correlation. Because this quasi-experimental technique has been described in some detail in several excellent papers (see Campbell, 1963; Kenny, 1975; Pelz & Andrews, 1964), the approach will only be summarized here.

In its essential form, cross-lagged panel correlation is a correlational method intended to test for spuriousness (Kenny, 1975), that is, to determine whether the relationship between two variables can be attributed to the causal effects of either, or to a third variable which produces causal effects on both.

Although the existence of a causal relationship is one that can never be established empirically (Blalock, 1964), the identification of variables that "produce" others is an essential task for researchers concerned with issues of organizational intervention.

Since the purpose of cross-lagged panel correlation is to establish causal inference by ruling out the possibility of spuriousness, it follows that the null hypothesis of this technique is "that the relationship between X and Y is due to an unmeasured third variable, and not to causation" (Kenny, 1975, p. 889). This hypothesis is tested by examining the relative strength of six correlations which are generated by two variables, each measured at two points in time (see Figure 6-5):

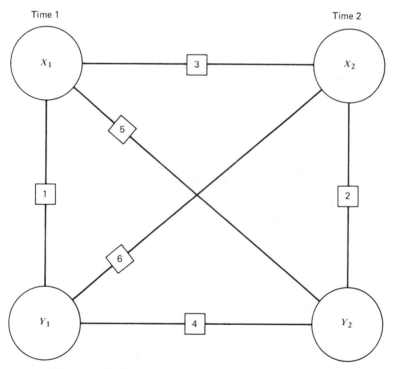

Figure 6-5   Cross-lagged panel correlation model.

two synchronous correlations (1 and 2); two autocorrelations (3 and 4) and two cross-lagged correlations (5 and 6).

It was originally suggested by Campbell (1963) that the cross-lagged differential could be used to establish the "relative preponderance" of causal relationships: "Where two data series correlate, e.g., annual Norwegian harvest yields and numbers of marriages . . . $r_{C_n \cdot E_{n+1}}$ should be greater than $r_{C_{n+1} \cdot E_n}$, where C stands for cause, E for effect" (p. 236). Campbell termed the lagged differential proposed in this example a *cross-lagged series correlation*. Such time series data are seldom available in the social sciences, but, by extension, the technique may be employed with panel data involving measurements made on the same individuals at two or more points in time. The basic concept in each case is a comparison of the lagged correlations with preponderant causation suggested by the greater of the two values. Thus, in the case of Figure 6-5, the value of $r_{X_1 \cdot Y_2}$ should exceed that of $r_{X_2 \cdot Y_1}$ if X "causes" Y.

Since the technique of cross-lagged panel correlation was first introduced, it has been used to study such diverse topics as mother–child relationships, motivation, interpersonal attraction, and international relations (Kenny, 1975). It is an intuitively appealing technique that can be employed in situations where the traditional apparatus of random assignment and experimental manipulation cannot be used.

At the same time, cross-lagged panel correlation is not without limitations. It is largely an exploratory strategy of data analysis whose applicability, like that of other models, depends on the correctness of its underlying assumptions. In practice, these conditions are difficult to meet, and Rogosa (1980) argues that even in an idealized situation the technique may not provide a sound basis for causal inference. He fails to identify a satisfactory alternative for detecting patterns of causal inference, but it is clear that conclusions based on cross-lagged panel correlation need to be interpreted with caution. As with other quantitative techniques, the blind application of a set of statistical procedures is unsound and findings must be compared with understanding derived from empirical observation and formal theory.

LIMITATIONS OF THE RESEARCH

Seashore and Bowers (1963), in their lucid report on an earlier field experiment, provided a number of possible arguments for the convenience of those who would dispute their findings. Like their study, our research has a number of inherent limitations; following are some of the principal weaknesses:

1.   Judgments concerning the effectiveness of the Quality of Work Life program were based partly on analyses internal to the Centerton plant. This design is stronger than the alternatives we were able to identify: a single group pretest–posttest design using Centerton alone, or a post-test only design using Baytown and Centerton as nonequivalent comparison groups. The quasi-experimental design we did employ still has a number of weaknesses, particularly those involving selection–maturation and selection–treatment interactions and differential regression. Although the analytical procedures we used were selected to minimize the possibility of misleading biases, the outcomes of quasi-experiments are inevitably more equivocal than those observed in true experimental designs.

2.   In this study, results are considered significant if they could have occurred by chance fewer than five times in 100; however, the large number of statistical tests performed increases the probability of chance findings.

3.   Cook and Campbell (1975) have questioned the traditional use of significance tests when programs, not individuals, have been assigned to treatment, and the general applicability of statistical tests is a subject of heated controversy (Morrison

and Henkel, 1970). Following Winch and Campbell (1970), however, the position taken here is that:

> It is very important to have a formal and non-subjective way of deciding whether a given set of data shows haphazard or systemic variation. If it is haphazard, there is no reason to engage in further analysis and to be concerned about other threats to validity; if it is systematic . . . the analysis is not concluded with the test of significance but is just getting underway. And we believe it is important not to leave the determination of what is a systematic or haphazard arrangement of data to the intuition of the investigator. (p. 26)

Thus the statistical tests which are reported should be regarded as evidence of systematic variation, rather than as conclusive "proof." It is expected that some researchers will choose to apply tests which are more stringent, whereas others will be more flexible in their examination of the data presented.

4. We began the chapter by citing the independent research design as one intended to meet the special requirements of a complex experiment conducted in the natural environment. It served this purpose, but, as detailed in Nieva and Perkins (1980), the third-party design was not without problems. In particular, the presence of a separate evaluation team may have altered the phenomena under study, or introduced another frame of reference. To the extent that this occurred, the results are not generalizable to settings without such third-party dynamics.

5. Conclusions are seldom based on a single, totally persuasive piece of evidence. Analyses typically attempt to integrate diverse data sets consisting of both qualitative and quantitative findings. Procedures for accomplishing these syntheses are complex, and our judgment may be questioned by those with differing perspectives—or by those with more plausible interpretations of the evidence we examined.

Chapter Seven

Implementation of the Quality of Work Life Approach

An intervention aimed at the somewhat abstract concept of a "good quality of work life" cannot be assessed without a clear understanding of the nature of the intervention. To use a medical analogy, it is necessary to know what the treatment was, how it was administered, who the actual recipients were, and in what "dosages" it was provided.

This chapter will examine the implementation of the Quality of Work Life program, assessing its impact from four perspectives. First, the intervention will be described from the vantage point of the observers who watched the unfolding of the consultant's program. Second, its impact will be discussed from the perspective of Centerton employees' ratings of the extent to which they were personally affected by the program. Third, the implementation will be described in terms of the contact between the consultants and Centerton employees. Finally, the question of goal attainment will be explored, that is, the degree to which Quality of Work Life intervention objectives were actually achieved.

These perspectives bear on the first two panels of the analytical model that guided the evaluation design (see Figure 7-
1). Observational data, taken from the site historian's notes,
describe the activities subsumed under the first panel of consultant intervention. The effect of these activities is assessed
with the use of questionnaire data about the consultants' personal impact on Centerton employees as well as the extent of
consultant contact. The second panel, achievement of Quality
of Work Life program goals, is analyzed using observational
data and the results of the Goal Attainment Survey.

At the conclusion of the chapter, we summarize our assessment of the program's impact and discuss problems encountered in its implementation. Individual and organizational
outcomes, such as productivity and satisfaction, are discussed
in Chapter 8.

THE INTERVENTION: OBSERVATIONAL DATA

Target Population

The consultants operated according to a tenet of intervention
theory that recommends starting at the top of the organization
(see Greiner, 1970). The project was given official corporate
sanction through the efforts of the Project Director, who presented the concept to a number of high-level executives. The
subsequent intervention focused consultation activities primarily, though not exclusively, on higher echelons of the organization. The managers and supervisors were seen as the
principal channels through which goals would be achieved.
According to the consultants, "success for the Quality of Work
Life program would be heavily dependent on the actions of the
managers and supervisors; they would have to provide the
opportunities and conditions for employees' participation"
(Consultant Final Report, 1976, p. 3).

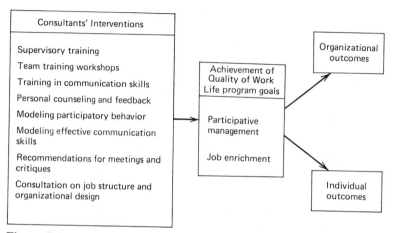

Figure 7-1   Analytical model employed in the Centerton evaluation.

Other data also suggest that the intervention was primarily focused at the top. For example, the Participant–Observer was introduced to the plant through a memorandum addressed only to the managers and supervisors. She received no further formal introduction, and consequently many of the lower level operators never understood her role or the reason she was at the plant.

It would be a misrepresentation, however, to say that the intervention team had no contact with the rank and file. The selection process, as well as the orientation and training program for new employees, included an introduction to the concepts of participation and work teams. In addition, the Participant–Observer occasionally joined work teams on the production floor.

Although the consultants concentrated their activities at the top level, their organizational focus was somewhat more complex. A greal deal of the consultants' attention was directed to the Production Department, where their efforts were largely confined to the managers. The Production Manager received extensive counseling in an effort to shift his managerial style from an authoritarian approach to one more in keeping with the avowed management philosophy. Much effort was expended to facilitate interpersonal relations at the managerial level, particularly the relationships between the Production Manager and the Fractionation and Filtration managers below him. Less attention was focused on the supervisors, and even less on the production operators.

The story was somewhat different within the Quality Assurance Department. As in the Production Department, the change agents spent a great deal of time with the unit manager, acting as sounding boards in free flowing discussions of administrative style. Unlike the Production Department, however, lower level employees were more intensely involved in the process of the Quality of Work Life intervention. The crucial difference was in the Quality Assurance Manager himself, a man totally committed to making participative principles work. In his commitment to the participative ideology, he organized frequent meetings to find solutions for intradepartmental problems and to discuss data from the researchers' questionnaires. The Participant–Observer was often asked to sit in as a process consultant on these occasions.

The intervention focused, then, almost completely on the Production and Quality Assurance departments. There was considerably greater participation by the rank and file in the latter department. Little effort was made to reach the Engineering and Maintenance Department, and many of their employees did not know of the intervention or the change agents. Also, although there was considerable awareness of the project in the Personnel and Accounting departments, there was little or no intervention activity focused on the departments as such—other than consultation between the change agents and the Personnel Manager.

Organizational Linkages: The Personnel Manager

One of the major elements in the strategy employed by the consultants was a commitment to working with and through the Personnel Manager. A consultant memorandum dated February 21, 1973 stated:

> The Centerton Personnel Manager will be exposed to opportunities that will enable him to assume—with full support from top line management—the guidance role in working out plans for staffing and organizing the Centerton plant—seminars, observations at companies that employed participative and job enrichment policies, selection and training, and compensation plans suitable to the increased responsibilities of the job enrichment approach.

Because the Personnel Manager was also expected to maintain the intervention after the departure of the consultants, he was directly involved in many of the intervention activities from the beginning.

The consultants worked closely with the Personnel Manager during the company's initial selection phase, drawing up recruiting and selection criteria and procedures. They also worked closely with him in designing the training programs for new employees. In addition, the Participant–Observer worked with employees and the Personnel Manager on matters such as advancement procedures and pay. The collaboration between the consultants and the Personnel Manager was designed to gradually minimize consultant involvement and to turn over the maintenance of the program to the Personnel Manager. The transfer of primary responsibility for the activities of the Quality of Work Life program was rapid; in fact, as early as the first new employees' training program, the Personnel Manager was almost completely in charge.

Level of Intervention Activity

For a number of reasons, the consulting team's approach started on a note of high intensity and then fell off abruptly, ending with a barely detectable level of activity. The initially intensive educational campaign, in which Centerton employees were introduced to Quality of Work Life concepts, was followed by intermittent efforts to help the organization put into practice the abstract concepts introduced in training. One production supervisor said: "Before we started up it was a high pressure thing. Since we've been in operation, we've been separated from the influence of that group—their influence was very minimal."

One of the reasons for the abrupt decline in activity was the departure of the Principal Investigator and the ambiguity surrounding the transfer of major responsibility for project maintenance to the Participant–Observer. Without a clear role definition, it was difficult for the Participant–Observer to undertake activities that entailed any significant intrusion into Centerton's already crowded list of priorities. In addition, a low consulting profile was consistent with the Participant–Observer's own style and preference.

Another related factor was the consultant's assumption that, toward the end of the intervention, the primary responsibility for implementing Quality of Work Life principles would rest on the organization itself. At this point, assistance would be provided by the consultants only when requested.

The effect of this consulting style, which was largely reactive rather than proactive, was that consulting priorities could not compete with the demands for time and energy generated by the start-up situation. As one of the supervisors put it: "There are so many pressures, the person who knocks hardest on the door gets the attention. The consultants weren't knocking hard enough."

There was disagreement about the appropriateness of this "low profile" strategy. Many of those involved in the program wanted to see a more active and aggressive stand from the consultants. The following comments were fairly typical:

> We should have gotten more guidance from the consultants. They should have told us that "these problems are likely to come up—be aware of them." With me you should probably hit me over the head and say, "Hey, do this because it's going to

buy you something." I have to be convinced. . . . I do think there could be . . . more aggressiveness.

However inappropriate this "low profile" may have been for others in the organization, it appeared to be just what the Plant Manager wanted. In a meeting with the consultants held to assess the impact of the intervention, the Plant Manager said:

Had you been too aggressive, I would have had difficulty dealing with you. There is a limit to what you can do—it is a counseling service. There were times I didn't want it. The more pushy you get, the more in the way it gets and the more turned off people get.

INTENSITY OF THE INTERVENTION

To assess the effects of an intervention such as the Centerton Quality of Work Life program, it is necessary that the intensity of "treatment" be determined, that is, the extent to which the experimental program was actually implemented. An analogy can be made here to the "manipulation checks" of laboratory experiments, which are conducted to document the levels of independent variables. The magnitude of the independent variables in the Centerton field experiment—the work of the consultants and the actual techniques used to implement the Quality of Work Life program—are discussed in this section.

Personal Impact of the Consultant Methods

In order to obtain an estimate of the degree to which the intervention had reached the employees at Centerton, employees were asked to indicate the *degree to which each method used by the consultants personally affected them,* on a response scale ranging from one (this did not affect me at all) to seven

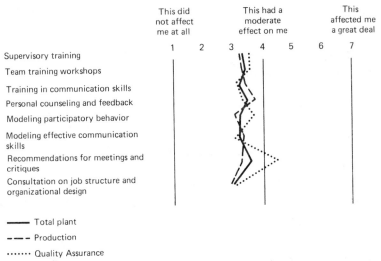

Figure 7-2   Perceived personal impact effects of consultant methods.

(this affected me a great deal). Figure 7-2 represents Centerton responses for the total plant and the Production and Quality Assurance departments separately. The majority fell below the midpoint of the scale; Centerton employees generally felt that they were personally affected by the consultants' methods and techniques to a less than moderate extent. Quality Assurance gave higher ratings to the consultants than did Production, although only the difference in ratings for "recommendations for meetings and critiques" was statistically significant.

Contact with the Consultants

A partial indicator of the intensity of the intervention is simply the amount of contact between consultants and clients. To get some sense of this interaction, Centerton employees were asked, "Approximately how much contact have you had with the consultants?" The response scale ranged from one (never)

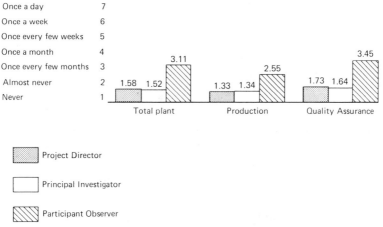

Once a day	7
Once a week	6
Once every few weeks	5
Once a month	4
Once every few months	3
Almost never	2
Never	1

Figure 7-3   Contact with the consultants.

to four (once a month) to seven (once a day). Figure 7-3 presents the pattern of responses to this question.

These responses suggest that the typical Centerton employee had relatively little contact with the Project Director and Principal Investigator. They had more contact with the Participant–Observer: On the average, they saw her about once every few months. The lack of contact between the consultants and Centerton employees was supported by comments made during the interviews. The following are representative:

> I haven't seen (the Participant–Observer) in four months. One time she said we would get together but we never did. I've been here almost a year and I have yet to have a consultant come to me as an individual, to sit down and ask, "How is it going? How is participative management working, or the quality of work life, or your relationships with co-workers?"

The departmental responses show that members of the consulting team had consistently greater contact with members of the Quality Assurance Department than with members of the Production Department. These differences were statistically significant for the Project Director but not for the Principal Investigator or Participant–Observer.

ACHIEVEMENT OF QUALITY OF WORK LIFE PROGRAM GOALS

Because of the consultant's strategy of concentrating on higher level managerial personnel, an average measure of contact is a limited indication of intervention "take." It does reveal differential impact, but it is insensitive to indirect change processes that affect lower level employees yet emanate from consultant–manager interactions. We therefore introduced another measure of "take" to assess the intervention impact: the extent of goal attainment.

It was expected that the previously described intervention methods would result in the accomplishment of a number of program goals. This section, which corresponds to the second panel in our analytical model (see Figure 7-1), describes our assessment of the extent to which these objectives were actually attained.

The analysis of goal attainment is divided into two parts. First, goals related to participative management are discussed. Second, those objectives concerning job enrichment objectives are examined. We chose this organization because, as will be discussed later, the success achieved in these two areas seemed to be markedly different.

To assess the degree of goal attainment, Centerton employees were asked to indicate the extent to which each of the objectives established by the consulting team had been met. Responses on the goal attainment questions ranged from one (this objective has not been achieved) to four (the objective has been achieved to a moderate extent) to seven (this objective has been achieved to a very great extent). Figure 7-4 presents the results of this survey.

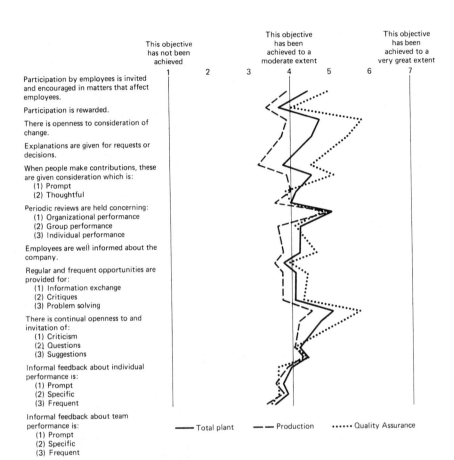

This objective has not been achieved

This objective has been achieved to a moderate extent

This objective has been achieved to a very great extent

Participation by employees is invited and encouraged in matters that affect employees.

Participation is rewarded.

There is openness to consideration of change.

Explanations are given for requests or decisions.

When people make contributions, these are given consideration which is:
  (1) Prompt
  (2) Thoughtful

Periodic reviews are held concerning:
  (1) Organizational performance
  (2) Group performance
  (3) Individual performance

Employees are well informed about the company.

Regular and frequent opportunities are provided for:
  (1) Information exchange
  (2) Critiques
  (3) Problem solving

There is continual openness to and invitation of:
  (1) Criticism
  (2) Questions
  (3) Suggestions

Informal feedback about individual performance is:
  (1) Prompt
  (2) Specific
  (3) Frequent

Informal feedback about team performance is:
  (1) Prompt
  (2) Specific
  (3) Frequent

—— Total plant   — — Production   ••••• Quality Assurance

Figure 7-4   Attainment of goals related to participation.

Participative Management Goals

For the plant as a whole, the data indicate that Centerton employees felt that most of the goals related to participative management had been achieved at a moderate level. Scores on "openness to consideration of change," and "continual openness to questions" were particularly high, but "rewards for participation" were seen as relatively low.

In the departmental data, Production responses tend to be lower than those of the total plant and below those of the Quality Assurance Department. In the majority of cases, Production employees tended to see the goals as having been achieved to a less than moderate degree, whereas Quality Assurance responses tended to be very slightly above the moderate level.

Statistically significant differences between departments were founded in the following seven areas:

1. Invitation to employee participation

2. Openness to consideration of change

3. Explanations given for decisions

4. Prompt consideration of suggestions

5. Thoughtful consideration of suggestions

6. Regular opportunities for information exchange

7. Openness to suggestions

In general, then, Centerton employees felt that the goals of participative management were only partially realized, and Quality Assurance tended to give significantly higher estimates of goal achievement than did Production.

Job Enrichment Goals

Like participation, job enrichment was an area in which the consultants had proposed a number of specific goals. The achievement of these goals was measured by the Goal Attainment Survey in a format similar to that used for participative management.

Responses on the goal attainment questions ranged from one (this objective has not been achieved) to four (this objective

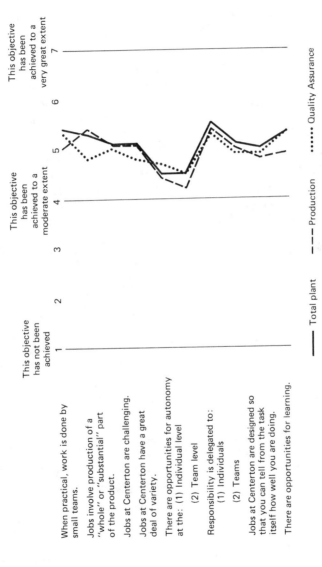

Figure 7-5 Attainment of job design goals.

155

has been achieved to a moderate extent) to seven (this objective
has been achieved to a very great extent). The total plant,
Production, and Quality Assurance responses to the questions
are presented in Figure 7-5.

This figure shows that employees at Centerton generally
felt that their jobs possessed the desired characteristics to a
substantially greater than moderate extent. The highest
achievement was found in the areas of "teamwork," "delegated
responsibility," "opportunities for learning," and "production
of a substantial part of the product." The figure also shows
that the responses of the two departments were highly similar.
Our analysis indicates that none of the departmental differences on the attainment of job design goals was statistically
significant.

PROBLEMS IN IMPLEMENTING THE QUALITY OF WORK LIFE PROGRAM

Some of the interviews give additional illumination to the
underlying reasons for the limited impact of the intervention.
In general, it appeared that the translation of the Quality of
Work Life principles into organizational realities was problematic. Relatively little work was done by the consultants beyond the propagation of general values, and Centerton employees were frequently left to interpret the management
philosophy in the course of day to day operations. In the words
of one employee:

> The general overview of the program was never really pre-
> sented—in other words, the employees had a vague idea as to
> what it was all about. But as to how they were to implement it
> on their own level as operators, they were left in limbo.

One of the supervisors voiced his confusion this way:

> The project was ill-defined from the beginning. First, it was
> participative management, then that was hushed up: "that is
> not the term we want to use." Then we got the word that PM
> (participative management) was only part of it. If it was only
> a part, why didn't we hear about anything else?

Clearly, stronger signals from the consultants would have
been welcomed by Centerton employees, most of whom were
receptive to the general principles of the intervention but were
at a loss as to how these abstractions were to be put into
practice. One manager said:

> The consultants were afraid to say, "No, you can't do this" or
> "that was a good piece of participative management." They
> seemed to be more of an independent observer like ISR. They
> should have grabbed people by their shirt collars—after all,
> they were being paid to help us along.

The need for more guidance became especially apparent in
later stages, when participants had drifted into more problems
than they could handle. One manager said: "We got ourselves
into a totally unstructured situation with no accountability. It
seems to me the consultants should have stepped in and said,
'Whoa, you're heading for disaster.' "

Of course, members of the organizations might have taken
more initiative in approaching the consultants for advice. During the stressful start-up period, however, these overtures simply did not occur. In addition, most employees were so new to
the Quality of Work Life ideas that they were unable to di-
agnose accurately what they needed. A manager expressed it
this way: "In reality, we did not know when to ask for help or
what to ask for, due to inexperience with Quality of Work
Life."

There also appeared to be a number of specific difficulties with individual facets of the intervention. For example, the training sessions, on which the consultants depended heavily for the dissemination of intervention principles, seemed to have limited applicability to the problems that supervisors encountered. One of the managers said: "We hit actual supervisory techniques light and never got out of the classroom into actual practice."

Supervisors also voiced similar opinions about the way the training sessions were handled:

> When we were going through the training sessions, no one ever asked if you understood. . . . "How did you perceive the project?" . . . I got the impression that this was just a show and tell.

> Those early training workshops were very superficial—very unrealistic. Even though the material we handled eventually came back, the experience we got was not good because it was set up so artificially and superficially.

Problems were also encountered with the counseling sessions, which had been given major emphasis by the consultants. On the positive end, some individuals clearly benefited. As one of the managers who received a good deal of counseling said: "With regard to me personally, they had pretty dramatic effects on my management style. . . . There's been a vast improvement in my approach to the people reporting to me."

However, many felt that the counseling sessions were not of much use—in particular, that they did not provide guidance regarding actual steps to be taken in the future. In the words of one supervisor:

> This counseling thing—I went up there with the expectation that I was going to find out what my weak points were as a supervisor or whatever and get some counseling about what I could do to improve myself as a person, and supervisor. Then I get up there . . . and he ended by saying something like, "Well, you look like a Saturn rocket about to take off" or some non-

sense like that. He didn't give me any counseling on what I'm
supposed to do next. All he did was to recommend about three
books to read. Reading something is all well and fine, but what
I wanted was practical suggestions on what to do.

From all indications, then, it appears that the intervention
was administered in relatively low dosages and had limited
effects on the day to day work lives of most Centerton employees. To use the terminology of laboratory research, "the treatment was weak." As one supervisor put it: "How much work
have we really done in the direction of Quality of Work Life?
How much organization was really put into it? As far as I'm
concerned, not that much."

Since the intervention appears to have been so limited, it
was unlikely to have had major effects on organizational processes and outcomes. However, Centerton did show signs of
progressing toward some Quality of Work Life goals. Many
Centerton employees felt that their opinions were heard in the
organization, that explanations were given for decisions, and
that there was an atmosphere open to considering changes in
the plant. The Plant Manager appeared to be reflecting the
views of most of the Centerton personnel when he said:

> We do have a good bit of participation, not only at the operator
> level, but at the supervisor and manager level—throughout we
> have this business of inviting people's comments, inviting sug-
> gestions, and considerately listening to their ideas.

Centerton employees also felt that their jobs possessed a
number of desirable characteristics. Work was done by small
teams, employees perceived their jobs to be challenging, and
employees felt responsibility for their work. Job rotation,
which was seen by the consultants as a mechanism through
which employees would have more varied and more challenging jobs, was also achieved to a reasonable degree in some
teams. One Production Operator described the process in his

group thus: "One person schedules work throughout the day on the worksheet; each job is rotated. It used to be that the supervisor did that, but now it's rotated and most people can do most things."

Goal attainment in participative management was less successful than in job enrichment, however, and our interviews shed light on why this was so. It appears that the consultants were indeed successful in disseminating the participative ideology and in creating the belief that, by operating according to its tenets, great things could be achieved. However, problems arose at the first efforts to put the participative theory into practice. It was difficult to put into operational terms what "participation" really meant, and to translate the concept into decisions about who was responsible for what and when.

Early on, participation began to be understood as "everyone having to decide everything." As one supervisor put it: "The impression I got when I first arrived was that everyone had to vote on everything." This simplistic understanding of participation as the involvement of everyone in everything may have created unrealistic expectations and subsequent frustration. Many of Centerton's problems were of a technical nature and required highly specialized expertise. Yet there was an implicit expectation that soliciting everyone's ideas on even those problems would result in a workable solution. One of the supervisors who recognized this problem said: "Most of our problems were at a level the operators couldn't solve since it takes a certain amount of knowledge to participate effectively." In addition, the notion of universal participation led to constant meetings to decide a great number of routine issues. Emphasis on these meetings took up a large proportion of valuable time and may have hindered individual decision making. A supervisor said:

> One of the problems was that the consultants came in and had so many team meetings that our decision-making ability was

impaired. Supervisors felt hindered in making decisions because it might not be the whole team's concept of need, and therefore decisions were not made.

Questions about the role of supervision in a participatively run organization were especially vexatious. The consultants' teaching on participative management was not sufficient to reconcile the principles of participation with the practice of "leadership." A number of supervisors understood the participative style to mean "majority rule," and felt stifled in their authority. Given the general directive to delegate responsibility downward, some supervisors felt stripped of their authority and began to see themselves as nothing more than "super operators."

Problems in the job enrichment area were, in some ways, parallel to the problems of participation. Again, the difficulty lay not in the basic acceptance of the idea, but in its application to actual practice. In many instances, employees were rotated through jobs for which they had been inadequately trained. The result was that many employees knew how to do a little bit of a variety of tasks, but only the supervisor had mastery over each one.

It is important to note, however, that the organization was better able to institutionalize the structural features of job enrichment than to adopt a system of participative decision making. The difficulty lay not in creating converts to the general idea of participation; rather, it lay in an inability to apply concepts in the context of Centerton's daily operations. Centerton employees needed, and did not seem to get, specific guidelines concerning what the concept of participation meant in terms of supervisors' behavior, task allocation, and decision making. A manager summed it up when he said: "We never said which decisions needed to be talked about, which things could be influenced, and so on. There were no 'parameters' on anything."

SUMMARY

Perhaps the implementation of the Quality of Work Life program can best be put into perspective by returning to the list of potential design features introduced in Chapter 1 (Table 1-1). Centerton did attempt to incorporate many of the elements we have seen in other high involvement settings. Its organizational structure was flat, with little hierarchy separating operators and technicians from the Plant Manager. Jobs were enriched, at least within the limitations of available technology, and the team structure was a cornerstone of the organization. Goals were set through a participative process that involved nearly everyone in the plant, and the selection of new employees was placed almost entirely in the hands of the supervisors responsible for the plant start-up. Finally, the Quality of Work Life program included extensive training in interpersonal skills; the reward system was keyed to skill levels of individual employees; and the physical structure reflected the egalitarian spirit of the organization. There were no choice parking spots for managers, and offices did not emphasize the trappings of rank.

At the same time, many potential features were excluded from the organizational design, and some features that were included seemed poorly articulated. The employee "communication meeting," for example, was a representative structure made up of employees who were selected by their peers. These meetings, which were led by the Plant Manager, offered a forum for raising troubling issues and exchanging information. But they in no way represented a participative council, and the hierarchical position of the Plant Manager was clear. In contrast, however, collaborative decision making prevailed during team meetings as supervisors invoked their power only with the greatest reluctance.

Job design was a central part of the intervention, and most work was enriched with elements of Hackman and Oldham's

(1974) core job dimensions. Yet the press for job enlargement resulted in a training overload, since operators were encouraged to learn new jobs before they felt comfortable with their first assignments.

The selection system was also problematic. The selection process was team centered, but the research described in Chapter 5 suggests that supervisors were lacking in many of the skills needed to make valid choices among applicants. They were also unable to provide a realistic job preview to job candidates since most supervisors were, themselves, so inexperienced.

Training deficiencies had an impact on other facets of the Quality of Work Life program. Interpersonal skill training was given heavy emphasis but little or no attention was paid to economic education. This meant that later, when employees were exposed to financial data about organizational performance, they saw little relevance.

Perhaps one of the greatest difficulties of implementation lay in the reward system. Compensation was indeed skill based, and employees felt pressured to expand their expertise. But the reward system was based entirely on individual performance, and there were no extrinsic incentives for team accomplishment. This inconsistency with the heavy team emphasis created internal friction. There were other difficulties with the design of the reward system as well.

The absence of any gain sharing or ownership plans for employees meant that participative management was frequently divorced from concerns about profitability. Employees thus had no direct interest in the financial performance of the organization, and many had little understanding of the economics of the industry. It is not surprising, therefore, that demands for a color television set for the break room could compete with pressing problems in plasma production.

Inconsistencies also occurred in the design of personnel policies. Procedures for disciplinary action were, for example, established through a time-consuming participatory process, and every effort was made to avoid terminating employees who had become part of the Centerton family. But employment security was affected by forces beyond the control of the Centerton Plant Manager, and a 2-week layoff—caused by fluctuating market dividends—raised serious questions about the company's commitment to a stable employment policy.

In summary, then, the Centerton Quality of Work Life program was implemented in a paradoxical way. Some features of a high involvement system were incorporated to the fullest extent imaginable. Other potential components were limited or nonexistent, and the result was an uneven, and sometimes incongruent combination of elements. New employees were indoctrinated with a number of behavioral science concepts, and supervisors made a concerted effort to practice the Quality of Work Life principles they had learned. But the pattern that emerges is generally one of limited impact, with systematic differences among departments in the "take" of the intervention.

Chapter Eight

Effectiveness of the Quality of Work Life Program

It was expected that the Quality of Work Life program would result in a number of attitudinal and behavioral changes. The anticipated effects examined in this chapter were selected for their centrality to the concept of "quality of working life." Some of these outcomes were explicitly identified by the consultants as intervention targets; others were derived from the literature describing environments exhibiting a high quality of working life.

The phrase "quality of work life" has been interpreted in various ways (see Katzell & Yankelovich, 1975; Walton, 1974). Suttle (1977) defines the quality of work life in terms of the extent to which individual needs are met by the organization and argues that:

> The quality of an individual's work life has been shown to affect many of his responses to his job. Improvements in quality of work life might lead, for example, to more positive feelings towards one's self (greater self-esteem), towards one's job (im-

165

proved job satisfaction and involvement), and toward the organization (stronger commitment to the organization's goals). They might also lead to improved physical and psychological health—fewer mental health problems and less inclination to become addicted to drugs or alcohol—and to greater growth and development of the individual as a person and as a productive member of the organization. Finally, a higher quality of work life can often lead to decreased absenteeism and turnover, fewer accidents, and higher quality and quantity of output of goods and services. (p. 9)

Although Suttle's conception is not definitive, we believe that his perspective provides a useful framework for examining outcomes that might reasonably be expected from a Quality of Work Life program. To measure the extent to which these outcomes occurred at Centerton, we selected six attitudinal variables: general work satisfaction, satisfaction with job facets (existence, relatedness, and growth needs), self-esteem, involvement, and organizational trust. The last attitudinal outcome, organizational trust, was chosen because of its particular significance in the Quality of Work Life program as implemented at Centerton.

In addition to these six attitudinal measures, two behavioral outcomes—absenteeism and turnover—are included in the analysis. Effects on organizational productivity are also discussed, although these data were particularly difficult to interpret. The 10 individual and organizational outcomes included in this chapter are shown in Figure 8-1, which depicts their position in the evaluation design.

To assess the extent to which these potential outcomes were achieved, we looked first at their immediate impact, that is, the effects observed during the most active stage of the intervention. In addition to these analyses, however, we searched for long-term effects. For this second assessment, we returned to Centerton over a year after the change agents had departed. At that time, a third questionnaire was administered, and a number of key organizational members were interviewed.

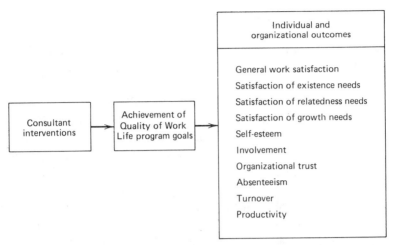

Figure 8-1   Analytical model employed in the Centerton evaluation.

Our strategy for assessing intervention effects varied, depending on the outcome in question. Behavioral measures—absenteeism, turnover, and productivity—were evaluated on the basis of time series comparisons. Intervention effects on attitudinal outcomes were assessed with the standardized change score analysis described in Chapter 6, supplemented with interview data, clinical observation, and time series comparisons when monthly Short Form data were available. Our change score analysis relied on the differential "take" of the Quality of Work Life program in the two Centerton departments and used departmental membership as a measure of treatment. In addition, to explore the possibility that beneficial effects of the intervention operated through direct contact with the change agents, consultant interaction was used as a second measure of treatment.

The strategy of using internal comparison groups is not the only one we might have employed. Although we were unable to collect longitudinal data from Baytown, we might have made inferences about intervention effects from cross-sectional comparisons of Baytown and Centerton. This procedure was, in fact, used by the consultants, who concluded that "the fact that Centerton scored significantly higher than Baytown on so many variables provides some evidence to the effect that the intervention may well have at least contributed to those outcomes" (Consultant Final Report, 1976).

Because of the myriad threats to validity inherent in a static group comparison design (Campbell & Stanley, 1963), we believe the Baytown evidence to be extremely weak. Nevertheless, we recognize the importance of providing multiple data sources, and we believe that no single perspective can adequately portray the results of such a complex field study. Consequently, later in this chapter we have included data comparing the Centerton and Baytown plants on our seven attitudinal measures, and we discuss Centerton's performance vis-à-vis three other new plants.

The chapter is divided into five major sections. In the first, we present our assessment of the immediate impact of the Quality of Work Life program, using data collected during the most active phase of the intervention. In the second section, we consider the possibility of long-term effects, based on our analysis of survey data collected over a year after the departure of the change agents. The third section compares Centerton's outcomes with those of the Baytown plant, and the fourth looks at Centerton's performance vis-à-vis several other new manufacturing plans. Finally, in the fifth part of the chapter, we summarize our views on the outcomes of the Centerton Quality of Work Life program.

IMMEDIATE EFFECTS OF THE QUALITY OF WORK LIFE PROGRAM

General Work Satisfaction

Job satisfaction has been studied extensively during the last 40 years. Research on the attitudes of individuals toward work has been motivated by several related interests. Initially, it was believed that satisfied workers were more productive employees, and satisfaction was pursued as instrumental to greater individual effectiveness. Later studies failed to find the expected satisfaction performance relationship (see Brayfield & Crockett, 1955; Vroom, 1964) and subsequent research suggests that the preponderant causal relationship is probably the reverse (see Lawler & Porter, 1967).

Job satisfaction continues to be an important concern, however, since individual satisfaction has been found to be related to absenteeism and voluntary turnover, both of which influence organizational effectiveness (Lawler, 1973). In addition, fundamental concerns about the quality of life in organizations, and increasing interest in noneconomic rewards (see *Work in America,* 1973), suggest that work satisfaction is a key criterion measure—independent of its impact on productivity.

Job satisfaction is of particular interest in the present research because of its central role in the Quality of Work Life program. As the consultants wrote:

> The following hypothesis of the study can be stated as follows: If an organization operates according to QWL guidelines . . . productivity and job satisfaction are likely to reach and be sustained at a higher level than would be achieved under traditional operating arrangements. (Consultant Final Report, 1976, p. 14)

Thus a measure of job satisfaction is important because of concerns about productivity, because of interest in the noneconomic rewards to be derived from work, and because of its explicit relationship to the Centerton Quality of Work Life program. Work satisfaction was measured using a 3-item scale designed to assess employees' overall satisfaction with their jobs.

The attitudes of those who responded to the assessment questionnaire declined significantly during the first assessment period. This downtrend is reflected in changes in the monthly Short Form item, "All in all I am satisfied with my job" (Figure 8-2). Figure 8-3 shows that the two Centerton departments followed roughly the same downward course.

When departmental membership was used as a measure of treatment, no significant effects on satisfaction were found. Similarly, we found no indication that interaction with the consultants had significant effects on general work satisfaction. In summary, we did not find any evidence that the Quality of Work Life program had an immediate impact on the work satisfaction of Centerton employees.

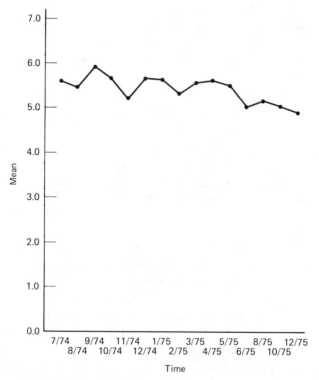

Figure 8-2 **Work satisfaction of Centerton employees: "All in all, I am satisfied with my job."**

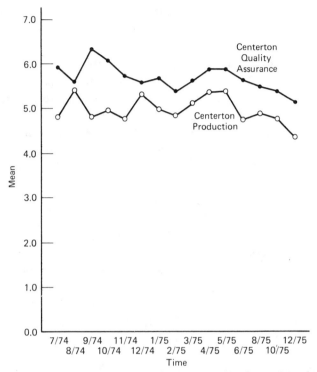

Figure 8-3   Work satisfaction of employees in Centerton Quality Assurance and Production departments: "All in all, I am satisfied with my job."

Satisfaction with Job Facets

In addition to overall job satisfaction, measures were included to tap attitudes about specific aspects of Centerton jobs. Later analyses revealed that employees tended to see these facets according to three principal groupings. These clusters correspond to the three dimensions of Alderfer's (1972) theory of human needs: (1) *existence* needs, concerned with security and material desires; (2) *relatedness* needs, concerned with desires for relationship and affiliation; and (3) *growth* needs, concerned with forces which impel a person to make creative or productive effects on one's self or environment. Results for each of these three measures will be discussed separately.

Satisfaction of Existence Needs. Material concerns were not a primary focus of the intervention, but fair pay and benefits were specifically cited as elements of a high quality of work life. In addition, employees expressed increasing concern about these issues as the study progressed. Individual attitudes toward basic existence needs were measured by a three-item scale encompassing pay, security, and fringe benefits. Like overall satisfaction, satisfaction with existence needs declined significantly during the first assessment period.

Our analysis of change scores provided no evidence that contact with the change agents had significant effects on employee satisfaction with existence needs, and no evidence was found that employees in the Quality Assurance Department experienced greater satisfaction of existence needs than those in Production. Consequently, we do not believe that the Quality of Work Life program significantly affected this outcome measure during the first assessment period.

Satisfaction of Relatedness Needs. Considerable effort was devoted to developing openness and trust among staff, and the team concept was stressed in the Centerton Quality of Work Life program. Consequently, the satisfaction of relatedness needs was an important criterion in our assessment of program outcomes. Attitudes toward satisfaction of relatedness needs were measured by a four-item scale that examined relationships with supervisors, and the respect and support provided by co-workers.

Satisfaction with relatedness needs declined slightly during the measurement period, but this decrement was not statistically significant. The standardized change score analysis provided no evidence that contact with the change agents had significant effects on employee satisfaction with relatedness needs, and there was nothing to suggest that membership in the Quality Assurance Department produced greater effects on relatedness satisfaction than did membership in the Production Department.

On the other hand, we were continually impressed by the employees' favorable comments about opportunities for affiliation. For example, one supervisor—who was generally critical of the consultants—stated: "There is a bond created among people during start-ups. It's closer than a family relationship. I love everybody here, my people especially. . . . It's not the money that keeps me, and certainly not the soft life." These attitudes were pervasive. Even when team members expressed strong dissatisfaction with their work, satisfaction of relatedness needs seemed high.

This apparent contradiction may result from the fact that one aspect of the Quality of Work Life program, the team structure, was effectively implemented in both the Production and Quality Assurance departments. Team membership, along with the shared trials of start-up, appeared to serve as a foundation for the satisfaction of relatedness needs. It was to be expected, therefore, that differential effects were not observed in departmental comparisons, and that relatedness needs were met even when other facets were unsatisfactory.

In sum, interview and observational data suggest that the Quality of Work Life program—especially the team concept—may have had positive effects on the Centerton employees' satisfaction of relatedness needs. It is impossible to distinguish this possibility from the effects of a common "baptism of fire" experienced during the start-up of any new organization, but we believe it is likely that the intervention did have positive effects on the satisfaction of relatedness needs.

Satisfaction of Growth Needs. Like relatedness needs, growth needs were closely related to the central philosophy of the Quality of Work Life program. As the consultants noted

(Consultant Final Report, 1976), the intervention was designed to achieve:

1. An environment that encourages continuous learning, training, and active interest regarding the job, and the product or service to which the job contributes. A setup that enables an employee to use and develop his personal skills and knowledge, which in turn affects his involvement and self-esteem from the work itself. (p. 96)

2. Provision of opportunities for continued growth, opportunities to advance in organizational or career terms. (p. 98)

Attitudes toward the satisfaction of growth needs were measured by a seven-item scale encompassing participation in decision making; the development of skills and abilities; the accomplishment of worthwhile goals; and other items instrumental to the fulfillment of higher order needs.

Satisfaction of growth needs declined sharply during the assessment period, and this decrease was highly significant statistically. As was true for other outcome measures, our analysis of standardized change scores provided no indication that contact with the consultants significantly affected satisfaction of growth needs or that membership in the Quality Assurance Department produced positive effects on employee attitudes. These results were generally consistent with other evidence, and we therefore conclude that the intervention had little immediate impact on the satisfaction of growth needs of Centerton employees.

Self-Esteem

Self-esteem, defined by Robinson and Shaver (1973) as "liking and respect for oneself which has some realistic basis" (p. 45), has been cited as an important index of improvement in the Quality of Work Life (see Taylor, 1973). In the context of the Centerton intervention, self-esteem was identified by the consultants as an individual difference variable expected to be enhanced by the Quality of Work Life program. Self-esteem was measured by a three-item scale encompassing attitudes toward one's self and the extent of self-satisfaction.

Our measure of self-esteem declined significantly during the assessment period. We found no evidence that membership in the Quality Assurance Department favorably affected self-esteem, or that contact with the consultants enhanced employees' self-concept. We found no interview or observational data to the contrary, and consequently, it does not appear that the Quality of Work Life project had immediate positive effects on the self-esteem of Centerton employees.

Involvement

There is reason to believe that participation in organizational decision making should lead to the internalization of organizational goals and behaviors—such as increased productivity, decreased absenteeism, and turnover—that are supportive of the organizational mission (Katz & Kahn, 1966). It is understandable, therefore, that organizations attempt to obtain an optimal level of employee involvement (Lawler, 1973); greater involvement in work was indeed an expected outcome of the Quality of Work Life program (Consultant Final Report, 1976).

Employee involvement at Centerton and Baytown was measured by a four-item scale encompassing the importance of work related events, and the extent to which individuals performed their jobs solely for financial compensation.

The involvement of Centerton employees declined during the assessment period, and this difference was statistically significant. As shown in Figure 8-4, these changes were consistent with increases in a component item of the involvement scale, "I don't care what happens to this organization as long as I get my paycheck." The departmental trends, shown in Figure 8-5, followed roughly the same course.

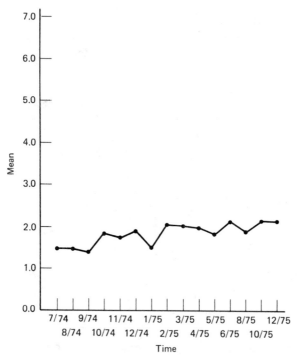

Figure 8-4 Involvement of Centerton employees: "I don't care what happens to this organization as long as I get my paycheck."

Although employee involvement declined during the assessment period, there was no evidence that these changes were engendered by direct effects of the Centerton Quality of Work Life program. Our standardized change analysis scores provide no indication that membership in the Quality Assurance Department significantly affected employee involvement, or that involvement was influenced by contact with the change agents.

Organizational Trust

A major share of the consulting intervention was devoted to activities intended to create a climate of trust among Centerton employees. If the Quality of Work Life program had succeeded in reaching this objective, therefore, we would have expected positive effects to be revealed in our survey measure of organizational trust. This variable was assessed with a five-item scale which dealt with the degree to which the employees felt that the company can be believed and trusted, and the degree to which the company was seen as taking advantage of the employees.

As shown by scores on the component item, "This organization cares more about money and machines than people," the level of trust declined significantly during the intervention period (see Figure 8-6). Both the Quality Assurance and Production departments indicated this same general course (Fig-

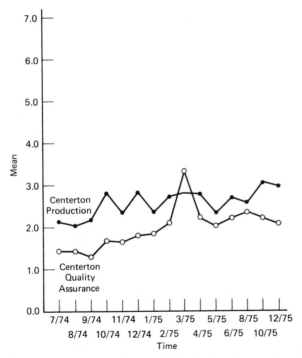

Figure 8-5   Involvement of employees in Centerton Quality Assurance and Production departments: "I don't care what happens to this organization as long as I get my paycheck."

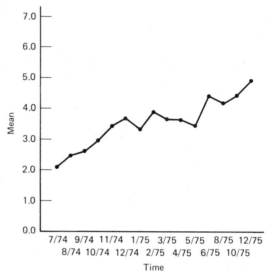

Figure 8-6   Organizational trust of Centerton employees: "This organization cares more about money and machines than people."

ure 8-7). Once again our change score analysis provided no indication that the decline in trust was associated with the intervention. Neither contact with the change agents nor departmental membership showed statistically significant effects on organizational trust.

Absenteeism

Absenteeism, particularly voluntary absenteeism, is a behavioral measure closely related to job satisfaction (Vroom, 1964). High absenteeism rates are associated with "organizational entropy" (Argyris, 1970), and Lawler (1973) observes that the costs of absenteeism are to be found in interrupted scheduling, increased fringe benefits, and overstaffing.

To examine the effects of the Quality of Work Life program on absenteeism, company personnel data were collected from April 1974 to February 1976. At this point, the organization changed its reporting procedures, and subsequent data are not comparable. (Because absenteeism was of interest primarily for its relation to employee satisfaction and alienation, only voluntary absences were reported.) As indicated by Figure 8-8, the plant wide rate rose from 1.8 percent at the beginning of the study, a rather low level, to 3.4 percent at the conclusion of the data collection. The average rate for this period was 2.1 percent. During the same period, the rate of absenteeism at Baytown was considerably higher (6.8 percent); the absenteeism rates in the Centerton Quality Assurance Department were lower than those in Production (Figure 8-9), and they did not follow the upward trend shown by the Production Department and the plant as a whole. It seems possible, therefore, that the Quality of Work Life program—which was more successful in the Centerton Quality Assurance Department—may have had some role in preventing the absenteeism increases found in other units of the Centerton plant.

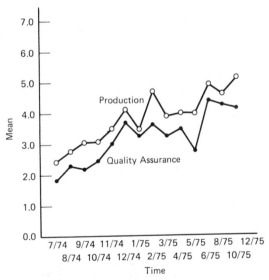

Figure 8-7 Organizational trust of employees in Quality Assurance and Production departments: "This organization cares more about money and machines than people."

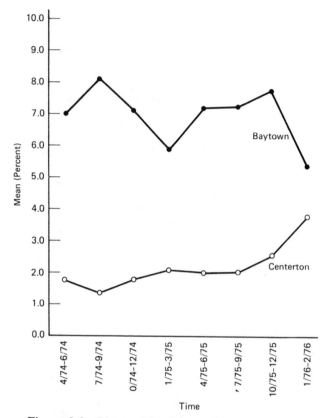

Figure 8-8   Plant wide absenteeism at Centerton.

Turnover

Turnover is one dysfunctional consequence of employee dissatisfaction with the working environment. As Lawler (1973) notes:

> Turnover is expensive because of the many costs incurred in recruiting and training replacement employees. For lower-level jobs, the cost of turnover is estimated at $2,000 a person; at the managerial level, the cost is at least five to ten times the monthly salary of the job involved. (p. 87)

Turnover is important, therefore, because of its cost to the organization and because it is correlated with the satisfaction of organizational members. And, in the context of a Quality of Work Life program, turnover is an important behavioral measure of success.

Unlike absenteeism data, turnover rates are reported with some consistency across time and organizations, and thus can be reliably compared with data from other settings. Aggregate turnover rates may, however, be artificially inflated by such

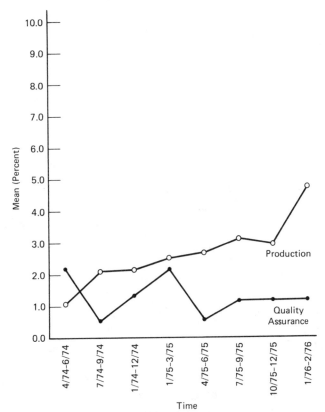

Figure 8-9   Quality Assurance and Production departments' absenteeism.

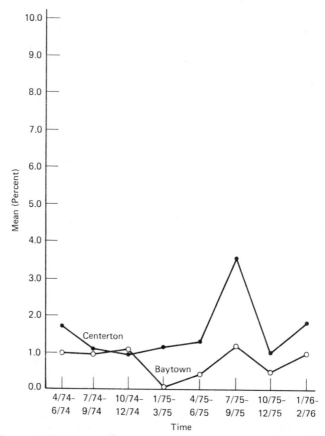

Figure 8-10   Centerton and Baytown total plant quit rates.

factors as market conditions that generate involuntary separations. To find a more valid behavioral indication of employee attitudes toward the organization, therefore, only voluntary turnover was used as a criterion in this assessment.

Two basic sources of data were used for comparison. First, nationwide figures were available for voluntary turnover in the pharmaceutical industry. Second, turnover rates in the state's chemical industry were available.

Turnover data were collected from April 1974 to February 1976. The average turnover rate at Centerton (see Figure 8-10) for this period was 1.58 percent and the average level at Baytown was 0.9 percent, but no consistent trends were observed in the data. As shown in Figure 8-11, the average rate at the national level (0.9 percent) is lower than that of Centerton; the average state rate is higher (3.0 percent). Both

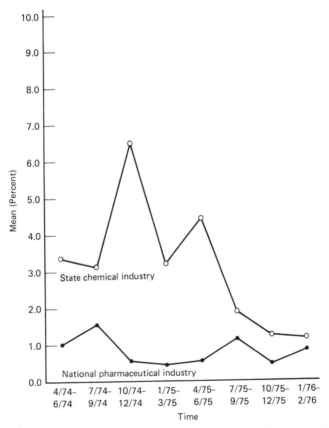

Figure 8-11   National pharmaceutical and North Carolina Chemical Industry quit rates.

rates decreased during the assessment period, and the state rate showed a stronger downtrend than the national data.

The average turnover rate of the Centerton Production Department (3.3 percent) was higher than that of Quality Assurance (1.9 percent). The Production rate decreased slightly (see Figure 8-12), while the turnover rate in Quality Assurance rose; however, neither change was statistically significant. These patterns are extremely difficult to interpret. In the Centerton Quality Assurance Department, where the Quality of

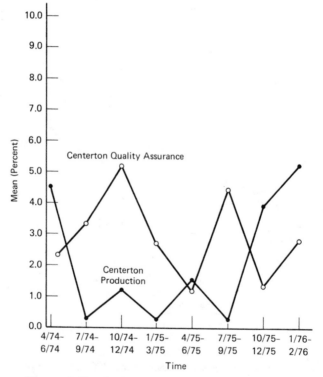

Figure 8-12   Centerton departmental quit rates.

Work Life intervention was most favorably received, the average rate was slightly lower than in Production, and the Centerton rate was lower than in the state chemical industry. On the other hand, the average turnover rate was lower in the pharmaceutical industry and at Baytown, and the Centerton rate rose during a period in which the statewide chemical rate declined. Because of the complex and contradictory nature of these turnover patterns, we believe they are not useful for making inferences about effects of the Quality of Work Life program.

Productivity

Increased productivity is cited as a frequent outcome of efforts to restructure the work environment (see *Work in America*, 1973; Glaser, 1976). Like job satisfaction, productivity was a critical outcome measure expected to be favorably affected by the Centerton Quality of Work Life program. Improved organizational effectiveness was also expected by the management of Crown Medical Specialties, and subsequently reported by the consultants as one of the positive outcomes of the intervention.

We had originally planned to collect a variety of production measures from both the Baytown and Centerton plants. With these data it was hoped that reliable inferences could be drawn regarding the impact of the intervention. Subsequent events, such as the development of technological differences between the plants and changes in Crown's management, rendered the original plan untenable. Nevertheless, some quantitative comparisons can be made, and the available evidence does permit some conclusions about the productivity of the Centerton plant.

Production Yields. The plasma production process described in Chapter 3 is an intricate one, requiring constant vigilance on the part of production employees. Lack of ability or attention and low motivation can have direct effects on product yield: the ratio of product output to input. Yield, therefore, is an important measure of effectiveness, which was carefully monitored at Centerton. Crown Medical Specialties planners chose existing Baytown yield levels as their initial goal for the Centerton plant, expecting that the Baytown levels would eventually be surpassed by the new, "state of the art" Centerton facility. Figure 8-13 shows the results of these efforts, indicating that the Centerton plant made steady progress in closing the gap between its performance and that of the Baytown facility. It is difficult, if not impossible, for us to evaluate the impact of the Quality of Work Life program on this learning course. However, as will be noted later, corporate

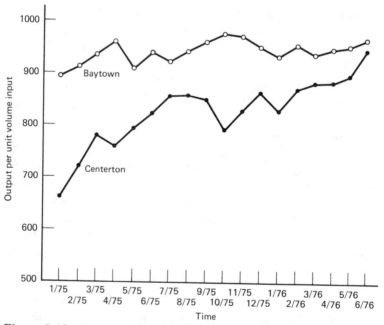

Figure 8-13 Plasma production yield at Centerton and Baytown.

management was pleased by the productivity yields of the new plant.

Production Volume. Because proprietary data relating to the total output of plasma are extremely sensitive, comparative volume levels at Baytown and Centerton could not be obtained. In addition, the output of each plant was largely a function of the market (which controlled sales of the finished product) and of the availability of raw material. Within the restrictive parameters of sales and procurement, however, we can say that the Centerton plant met or exceeded corporate projections for production volume levels.

Speed of Start-Up. Plasma fractionation was originally scheduled for March 1974. Owing to unseasonal rains and contractor difficulties, building construction and equipment installation were delayed and production was not begun until June 1974. Allowing for this initial delay, however, Centerton kept pace despite the adversities of the start-up period. As the Director of Manufacturing Technology and Procurement for Crown stated in 1976:

> Government qualification of the plant and the first major product line was made in accordance with the original schedule (revised to accommodate the March to June slippage). Production and qualification of the second major product line also met schedule. Plant expansion and installation of additional equipment for bringing it to planned production capacity was accomplished earlier this year about 30 days ahead of schedule.

Effects of the Intervention on Productivity. Centerton's production progress was generally considered successful by corporate planners, but the role of the Quality of Work Life project is unclear. The concept of participative management was largely rejected in the department that was most directly responsible for production and, in December 1974, the Plant

Manager attributed delays in production to problems with the Quality of Work Life program. Another key manager commented in early February 1975:

> Our priorities have changed now—we're concerned about surviving. Now I say, "Screw it," I've got to get the job done . . . [Participative Management] has been shelved . . . PM means that in many cases, I'm making the decision and then getting feedback later on. If I think I have the information, I make the decision.

At the operator level, production employees were largely unaware of the Quality of Work Life project or, if they had heard about it, felt it had been disregarded: "I feel like we were sold a lot of bull—now that they've got us they don't care what the employees think." Another stated: "All we heard from the beginning was teamwork and participative management—but it was all talk and no action."

At the managerial level, those most closely involved with production said little that was favorable about the contribution of the Quality of Work Life project to Centerton productivity. One felt that communication had been improved, but the general result of the intervention was negative.

> My dissatisfaction with things at the plant level didn't develop until we got into production . . . that was the point where decisions had to be made and I couldn't make them because we had to vote on everything . . . I think [the consultants] helped bring about a breakdown in regards to individual . . . accountability.

In sum, the Centerton production record appears to be strong. Yet most of those with whom we spoke seemed to feel that the organization had succeeded in spite of, rather than because of, the Quality of Work Life project. In addition, the fundamental rejection of broad participation by the Production Manager militates against our attributing production achievements to the enactment of Quality of Work Life principles.

LONG-TERM EFFECTS OF THE QUALITY OF WORK LIFE PROGRAM

In January 1977 we returned to Centerton for a third data collection effort. This follow-up was designed to monitor the development of the Centerton plant as it evolved into a mature organization and to identify any long term effects of the Quality of Work Life intervention. It was a particularly interesting comparison since it came over a year after the change agents had left the site. Thus, it represented a chance to observe any attitudinal changes that had occurred after their departure.

As shown in Figure 8-14, the outcome variables appear, in the long run, to have returned to levels very close to those of T_1. The measures that declined significantly from T_1 to T_2 rose from T_2 to T_3 although none of these changes is statistically significant.

When intervention effects were examined using the T_1 to T_3 measurement interval, two significant changes were found. First, organizational trust was related to departmental membership at Time 1, but not at the follow-up, suggesting a negative treatment effect. Second, when contact with the change agents was used as the treatment variable, one significant effect was found: Whereas satisfaction of growth needs was positively related to T_1, it was negatively related to T_3, that is, the more contact with change agents, the less satisfied Centerton "veterans" were with opportunities to satisfy growth needs.

For the most part, however, the period following the official termination of the Quality of Work Life intervention revealed general stability at Centerton. The new organization was meeting its production goals. Among the outcome variables, there was a pattern of consistent, though statistically insignificant, improvement for all the variables that had decreased significantly in the T_1–T_2 period. These changes portend an optimistic picture for Centerton, and suggest future recovery from the low levels found at T_2.

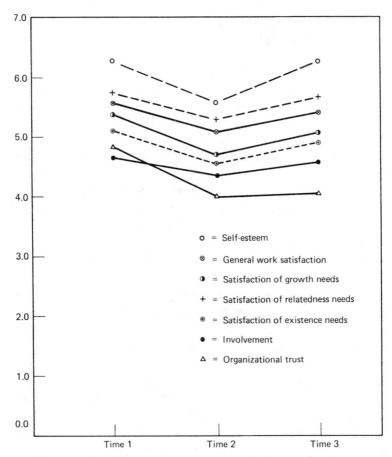

Figure 8-14   Changes in outcome variables at Centerton.

We believe that this apparent pattern of recovery can be attributed to the process of maturation and stabilization at the Centerton plant. With time, technological problems were brought under control, and many of the difficulties in the sociotechnical system became manageable. By our third measurement, the frenetic pace of the start-up days had relaxed considerably. It seems reasonable to predict that a similar upswing in attitudes might be found in most new plants as they "settle down." Because so little research on new plants has been done, this point cannot be substantiated; it must be taken as considered speculation.

It is difficult for us to explain the apparently detrimental effect of membership in the Quality Assurance Department on organizational trust. It seems likely, however, that the negative relationship between contact with the consultants and satisfaction of growth needs may reflect the impact of unmet expectations. That is, those who had the greatest exposure to Quality of Work Life principles were also most susceptible to disappointment when their ideals were not met.

In sum, the third-wave data do little to alter the basic conclusions reached after analysis of the T_1 and T_2 data. For Centerton, generally, it was a period of relative stability with some degree of improvement from the lows found at our second survey. And there was little in the data to suggest a positive "sleeper" effect on the part of the intervention.

COMPARISONS WITH BAYTOWN

Sensitive assessment of the Centerton experience required the balancing and integration of qualitative and quantitative evidence relating to each outcome measure. The task was a complex one, and the analytical process required a healthy measure of inference and judgment.

Alternative analytical procedures might have led to different conclusions about the outcomes of the Centerton Quality of Work Life program. The change agents, for example, argued that comparisons with Baytown should be used as evidence of favorable intervention effects. In fact, from the perspective of the consultants, these comparisons showed that the Quality of Work Life program "saved the plant."

A comparison between Centerton and Baytown (see Table 8-1) does show that, at T_2, Centerton scored significantly higher on four attitudinal measures: satisfaction of relatedness needs, satisfaction of growth needs, involvement, and organizational trust. There were no significant differences on measures of general work satisfaction or self-esteem. For behavioral measures, Centerton's absenteeism levels were lower than Baytown's, a favorable comparison, yet Centerton's rates were higher for turnover. Production levels were lower at Centerton during the period for which data are available.

If we had relied on these static comparisons to make inferences about treatment effects, then we would have concluded that the Quality of Work Life program had positive effects on involvement, trust, satisfaction of relatedness and growth needs, and absenteeism. No discernible effects would be identified for general work satisfaction, satisfaction of existence needs or self-esteem. Unfavorable effects would be inferred for turnover and productivity.

Table 8-1 Comparison of Outcome Measures for Centerton and Baytown*

	Plant	
Measure	Centerton	Baytown
General work satisfaction	5.31	4.98
Satisfaction of existence needs	4.64	4.46
Satisfaction of relatedness needs	5.50†	5.07
Satisfaction of growth needs	4.78†	4.04
Self-esteem	5.90	5.85
Involvement	4.51†	4.19
Absenteeism (percent)	2.1	6.8
Turnover (percent)	1.58	0.9

Note: Response scale runs from 1 to 7.

* Attitudinal measures were taken at T_2, December 1975.
Behavioral measures were averaged over the period from April 1974 to February 1976.

† Statistically significant difference.

The problem with this strategy is perhaps clearest in the case of productivity. Drawing conclusions about intervention effects from this measure would be clearly inappropriate since a new plant does not immediately produce at the rates it will later achieve. The effects of learning must be considered, and the appropriate method of comparison would be to find another plant facing similar start-up challenges.

This problem is not, however, restricted to productivity data alone. Unfortunately we do not have a model for predicting, for any measure, expected effects of maturational processes. Our data on long-term effects (see Figure 8-14) suggest a V shape somewhat like that typically observed for employees as a function of time in job. But data on new organizations are too sparse to generalize from this pattern.

This lack of a theoretical "template" is a troubling problem even when time series data are available, and it is even more serious when only cross-sectional, Time 2 data can be analyzed. A post-test only, nonequivalent comparison group design, or "static group comparison," is particularly vulnerable to validity threats arising from selection and mortality.

For example, it is possible—perhaps even probable—that the recruitment program selected a group of employees who were systematically different from those at Baytown. This is certainly true on the dimension of ethnicity, and it may well be true for other measures as well.

The possibility of selective mortality, or differential dropout, is another concern that cannot be dismissed. To use a classic, if sexist, example:

> When . . . studies show freshman women to be more beautiful than senior women, we recoil from the implication that our harsh course of training is debeautifying, and instead point to the hazards in the way of a beautiful girl's [sic] finishing college before getting married. (Campbell & Stanley, 1963, pp. 12-13)

Thus it is true that Time 2 comparisons with the Baytown plant generally favored Centerton, but these descriptive data do not address the central question of Quality of Work Life program effects. There are simply too many competing, plausible explanations for differences in these data.

Other problems arise if a simple case study design is used to compare Time 1 and Time 2 scores for the total plant. We would not, for example, attribute the T_2 to T_3 decline of outcome measures to the Quality of Work Life program, nor the T_2 to T_3 increase to the departure of the change agents. Again, competing explanations, such as organizational maturation, prevent us from making these inferences.

The ideal comparison would, of course, involve another new plant identical to Centerton on all relevant variables. Unfortunately, these data do not exist; in fact, there are almost no quantitative data on the effectiveness of most of the new Quality of Work Life plants. Some of these organizations have been studied by outsiders, however, and shown to have positive results.

COMPARISON WITH OTHER HIGH INVOLVEMENT ORGANIZATIONS

The Topeka plant of General Foods has been studied by Walton (1972), and by Jenkins and Lawler (1981). Both studies have found low absenteeism, low turnover, low production costs, and high employee satisfaction. Unfortunately, the Topeka plant is the exception as far as public data on organizational effectiveness are concerned. Comparable data simply are not available on most other new Quality of Work Life plants. But there is a good deal of circumstantial evidence that most, if not all, are highly successful in economic terms, and in the quality of work life provided for employees. For example, Procter & Gamble's new plants have been closed to researchers because of their belief that their approach provides a competitive advantage which they don't wish to share. It is also interesting that most corporations that have tried one new plant have gone on to try others (e.g., Procter & Gamble and General Motors). This would seem to indicate that they are meeting with some success. Finally, it is interesting that the demand from other companies to visit new design plants is great. Some of those that allow visitors even charge for tours.

Overall, we do not think that the Centerton start-up process was as successful as most of the other new design plants. Any comparison between Centerton and other new Quality of Work Life plants, however, must be very tentative because it is one of the first plants to have been studied in depth. It may be that if other start-ups were examined in similar detail, equivalent problems would surface. Given the available data, however, Centerton seemed to suffer more than its fair share of problems in its effort to implement participative management. In particular, our visits to other new plants revealed the following:

1. Few had abandoned or even considered abandoning participative management. We have heard of only one new plant (a Rockwell plant in Michigan that was started with the cooperation of the UAW) which has done so.

2. The members of other plants focused on further developing their systems and anticipating second generation issues.

3. They all talked about low absenteeism and turnover rates.

4. They all talked about how their productivity and quality exceeded traditional sister plants manufacturing the same products.

5. They all talked about the importance of helping other plants learn to operate the same way they did, and felt they could never manage in a traditional manner again.

Table 8-2   Mean Scores* in Four New Plants

	Organization			
Item	Centerton	X	Y	Z
All in all, I am satisfied with my job.	5.3	5.7	5.8	5.8
I often think about quitting (high scores are undesirable).	3.3	2.5	2.1	2.5
I get a feeling and personal satisfaction from doing my job well.	6.4	6.2	6.3	6.3
How much challenge is there on your job?	5.0	5.6	N/A	N/A
How satisfied are you with the chances you have to take part in making decisions?	4.8	5.6	N/A	N/A
My supervisor encourages subordinates to participate in important decisions.	4.7	5.2	5.1	5.2
What happens to the organization is really important to me.	6.1	6.1	6.2	5.9

* Response scale runs from 1 to 7.

Table 8-2 presents additional data comparing Centerton to other new plants. Each plant was measured at a stage of development comparable to the T_3 point in Centerton's history. They all are relatively small manufacturing plants owned by large corporations, and thus provide relevant benchmarks.

The measures were chosen because they highlight the general pattern we found in comparing the four plants. The other three plants are similar to each other, and are all considered to be "very successful" by their companies. There are some clear but not terribly large differences between Centerton and the other three plants. Centerton's employees are somewhat less satisfied, feel they have less challenge, and feel their supervisors are less inclined to encourage them to participate in decisions. On the other hand, there are no significant differences in how much satisfaction people get from doing their jobs well or in how much they are interested in what happens to the organization. This pattern is in accord with our conclusion that the Centerton start-up was somewhat less successful than that of other high involvement plants, but was certainly not a failure. Indeed, the scores in Table 8-2 are relatively high in an absolute sense, indicating that—despite lower levels of participation—a generally positive work attitude exists at Centerton.

These "new plant" data are not conclusive, and, indeed, we do not believe that any single comparison can be. But they are generally consistent with our other quantitative analyses, interviews, and observational data.

SUMMARY AND CONCLUSIONS

Our judgments about outcomes of the Quality of Work Life program, based on these data, are summarized in Table 8-3. We believe that the intervention contributed to the satisfaction of employees' relatedness needs, and that it also may have had a positive effect on absenteeism. It is also conceivable that the Quality of Work Life program may have increased productivity and decreased turnover, but these data are too am-

Table 8-3   Outcomes of the Centerton Quality of Work Life Program

Outcome Measure	None	Mixed or Ambiguous	Positive
General work satisfaction	X		
Satisfaction of existence needs	X		
Satisfaction of relatedness needs			X
Satisfaction of growth needs	X		
Self-esteem	X		
Involvement	X		
Organizational trust	X		
Absenteeism			X
Turnover		X	
Productivity		X	

biguous to interpret. Finally, we could find no evidence that the program made a direct contribution to general work satisfaction, satisfaction of existence needs, satisfaction of growth needs, self-esteem, involvement, or organizational trust.

It is important to recognize, however, that our formal assessment began after the intervention had begun, and it focused on the differential impact of practicing a set of behaviors associated with the concept of a high quality of working life. Viewed from this perspective, the goal accomplishment discussed in Chapter 7 seemed to have a rather limited impact on measures of outcome.

But it is also clear that Centerton is a very special kind of organization. Much of the qualitative data collected by the observers suggest unusual dedication, as exemplified by the following poem written by one enthusiastic employee.

"My Impression of Centerton"

My job at Centerton is very nice
I thank my God not once but twice

The Christian-hearted people there
Are different than you find just anywhere

We use our bodies, most every part
And thank God from the bottom of our heart

A variety is in it, we all share
Trying to be careful, for we really care

There is a life at the end of our task
That's why I pray to God to ask

That He will help everyone
To do their job and then their fun

Now for our boss, I'll have to say
Tony, you're a great guy
And have a nice day

'Twas written by one, but comes from all
So let's stick together so our department won't fall.

Said another way, the ethos of the organization was clearly special, and we believe that the intervention contributed to this perspective on the role of the individual in the work environment. As a result of the Quality of Work Life program, managers were exposed to a set of influential ideas, and they responded enthusiastically. This enthusiasm was blunted by the difficulty of translating their ideals into practice, and the project fell short of its initial goals. But there were some positive effects, and the experiement made a significant contribution to our understanding of new organizations and the quality of life at work. The next chapters draw on these learnings, extending our thinking on the Centerton experience to explore implications for the creation of other new organizations.

PART FOUR

SUMMARY AND CONCLUSIONS

Chapter Nine

Designing of High Involvement Organizations

The Quality of Work Life program at Centerton began with high hopes for the development of a successful high involvement plant. At the end of our formal study many of these hopes were gone or had changed. The plant was operating successfully in many respects, but the design envisioned at the outset no longer existed. In its place was a structure better suited to the needs of its employees, the constraints of its technology, and the demands of its corporate environment. In this chapter we will first focus on the problems that Centerton encountered in installing the high involvement design. We will then comment on how these problems affected the success of the Quality of Work Life program. Finally, we will examine the implications of the events at Centerton for the high involvement plant concept in general.

Problems at Centerton

As we have seen, Centerton encountered a spate of problems in implementing their Quality of Work Life programs. Some of these were specific to the unique situation at Centerton, but others are typical of high involvement plants. We will first consider those problems that are Centerton specific, and then turn to those that seem to be more general. It should be noted, however, that these problems are both complex and interrelated. Although discrete problems have been identified for purposes of explication, these problems clearly did not exist in isolation.

Inadequate Specification of the Management Style. The Centerton Quality of Work Life program was begun as a general philosophy of management that frequently lacked concrete form. It is true that some aspects of the intervention, such as team organization, were clear from the beginning. But it was not until February 1975—a year after production employees were first hired—that the Participant–Observer developed a comprehensive statement describing what an effective Quality of Work Life program might look like at Centerton. Prior to this statement, the form of the Quality of Work Life program was largely restricted to abstract principles which managers and supervisors found difficult to implement.

As one manager commented:

> The consultants caused us a lot of frustration. They convinced us it should work, but they weren't very effective in showing us how to make it better. And they didn't do any better than we did in analyzing where we were having problems. They took a passive role in saying, "We're here . . . ." Even when we did go to them, it was the same thing every time: "Get people involved."

General prescriptions of "involvement," "job enrichment," "open communications," and "good interpersonal relationships" failed, however, to provide a sufficiently concrete structure to guide the daily activities of Centerton employees. Even the general principle of participation, which was seen as the cornerstone of the Quality of Work Life program, lacked definition throughout much of the intervention.

Initial training sessions, for example, stressed a style of group problem solving which was interpreted by most participants as consensus decision making, or "collective wisdom." Pressures of the start-up situation militated against the exclusive application of this management approach, and an Institute Social Research report in March 1974 described a shift in the philosophy of the organization:

> Rather than a purely participative group system of management, the sentiment seemed to favor a style of organization characterized by Likert as "consultative," in which employees' recommendations are given a full hearing—but the final responsibility for decision making clearly rests with the work group supervisor.

The Principal Investigator disagreed with the report, contending that:

> In my view, the Centerton management team is somewhere in-between the consultative approach and the participative group system of management. Some members of the management team lean more toward the consultative style and some more toward the participative management approach. Some use a combination of the two, or use one at times.

In retrospect, however, it seems clear that a general shift toward consultative management had begun. But many supervisors continued to emphasize participation as a sort of religious philosophy in which autocratic heretics ran the risk of excommunication. Such a dogmatic application of participative principles was frequently ill-suited to the exigencies of the start-up situation, but more sophisticated contingency approaches (see Tannenbaum & Schmidt, 1973; Vroom & Yetton

1973) were never effectively communicated. Supervisors thus seemed unable to find a leadership style appropriate to the complex problems they faced.

In the early stages of the intervention, for example, the poorly defined boundaries of participation left many supervisors trying to involve employees in almost every aspect of decision making. A number of Centerton employees were frustrated by the failures of consensus decision making, yet they still aspired to the participative philosophy they believed the consultants had endorsed. One supervisor remarked:

> The trouble was that everybody got the idea that every decision had to be made by everybody. Then, someone would say, "Why don't you, the supervisor, make the decision—don't ask everybody." Others would say, "Why didn't you ask me?" There has to be a balance.

Under the pressure of time, however, Centerton supervisors did occasionally reject the idea of unqualified participation. The Plant Manager described one such incident:

> [The Principal Investigator] wanted supervisors to get involved in designing the training program for new employees. The supervisor said, "You take care of it; we don't have the time to participate in everything." [The Principal Investigator] was shocked!

The universal application of participative principles has seldom been endorsed, of course, even by the most enthusiastic proponents of collaborative decision making. Rensis Likert, for example, an early advocate of group-centered decision making, writes:

> It is essential that the group method of decision making and supervision not be confused with committees which never reach decisions or with "wishy-washy," common-denominator sorts of committees about which the supervisor can say, well, the group made this decision and I couldn't do a thing about it." Quite

the contrary! . . . The superior is accountable for all decisions, for their execution, and for the results. (Likert, 1967, p. 51)

The consultants later clarified their position on the boundaries of effective participation. At the conclusion of the project, they emphasized the importance of matching leadership style with contextual considerations and were surprised that participative philosophy had been misinterpreted. But the misunderstanding that pervaded all levels of the organization suggests that the consultants' concept of decision making was frequently misinterpreted by Centerton employees.

It appears that this problem resulted partly from the relative inexperience, even naiveté, of the Centerton managers. In the other plants we visited, consultants' ideas were quickly tempered by supervisors who were able to view outside ideas as a starting point for discussion. At Centerton, managers often lacked the experience to reshape unworkable proposals. At least initially, they seemed to embrace Quality of Working Life principles—which were presented as scientific "truths"—with uncritical acceptance. It was only later that they were able to adapt the consultants' ideas to fit their special needs.

One other point is worth noting here. In many of the other plants we visited, the management team was assembled months before construction began so that they could develop their management approach. The Centerton management had no such opportunity, and this seemed to contribute to their problems. The Plant Manager later reflected:

It was like playing the Superbowl with just a few days of practice. We came here from all over the company to play the game, and we had never had a chance to practice together before. We learned in a live situation.

In any case, one thing is clear: no one seemed to have a complete vision of how Centerton should have operated and, as a result, the early days were spent groping for a management structure and style.

Absence of an Integrated Intervention Strategy. The systemic properties of organizations cannot be ignored if change efforts are to succeed (Katz & Kahn, 1966). Modifications in one part of the system reverberate throughout, and successful change programs must take account of the need for integrated, coordinated strategies. As the Project Director—citing the experience of the Volvo plant—commented at the conclusion of the Quality of Work Life program:

> It is when we accept that change requires a total system approach, a package of activities introduced over time, that we increase our chance of success. The package or system would include delegation of responsibilities, job enlargement, job enrichment, . . . changes in the physical environment, and so on. What we call an integrated "social-technical administrative" approach increases the chances of success—so that one thing has to tie into another.

In actual practice, however, this integrated package often failed to materialize. Considerable effort was initially spent in facilitating openness and trust, increasing communication, helping employees confront problems directly, and in personal counseling. But the orchestration of these efforts—in the absence of clear specifications regarding what a high quality of work life would look like—was lacking.

Under these conditions, much of the actual intervention was concentrated at the individual level, where specific problems and disagreements were frequently the target of consultation. This was particularly true of the Participant–Observer, on whose shoulders rested de facto responsibility for implementing the Quality of Work Life philosophy. The consultants describe her method in their assessment of the intervention:

The Participant–Observer's style of intervention was to work with individual managers and supervisors, and occasionally with a departmental supervisory group, making observations, giving feedback to them, suggesting alternative ways to doing things, and offering resourceful help for system development. The choice of a less outspoken, individual-centered style resulted from personal preference, awareness of her "guest" status in the organization, and a sensitivity to the substantial pressures managers and supervisors were experiencing from the time delays in getting into production, with resulting exacerbating corporate financial dilemmas. (Consultant Progress Report, 1976, p. 44)

It is not certain that a more aggressive approach would have succeeded, and this unobtrusive style was consistent with the goal of promoting client autonomy. But uncertainty about the consultant's expectations, coupled with pressures to solve immediate problems, meant that the Quality of Work Life program was frequently ignored by harried managers.

The decision to rely heavily on individual level interventions was, moreover, inconsistent with the goal of producing system wide change. As Katz and Kahn (1966) observe: "The major error in dealing with problems of organizational change, both at the practical and theoretical level, is to disregard the systematic properties of the organization and to confuse individual change with modifications in organizational variables" (p. 390). Yet the actual work of the consultants—as distinguished from their formal goals—was largely directed toward individual growth and development. A supervisor who viewed the Quality of Work Life program favorably commented: "Individual counseling was good, but group sessions were less good. The supervisory training was the least effective." Another stated: "I see the consultants as a washout—The only thing they ever did constructive for me was individual counseling . . . but there was no follow-up."

This distinction between individual and systemic change was noted by another manager, who felt that he had personally benefited from some aspects of the Quality of Work Life program, but that the organization had not: "I think there's been a vast improvement in my approach to the people reporting to me . . . but I think plant-wide they helped screw things up." Individual counseling was, further, limited to a few individuals—primarily those at the supervisory level. It is therefore not surprising that little impact was felt throughout the plant.

As the evaluators interviewed team members at lower levels of the organization, this lack of contact became increasingly apparent. One employee, for example, had been with Centerton for over a year and had never heard of the consultants. The following comments are representative:

> I didn't know what she was doing. Sometimes she came and helped out. I never saw anyone else—[the Principal Investigator] maybe once, but I never spoke to him. I didn't know what she was asking questions for.

> I thought she was working with management, to see how we were doing. There were so many different ones passing through.

> I don't think [the Participant–Observer] was interested in our level—she concentrated on people higher up.

Even among the supervisors, however, contact was frequently minimal. As one complained:

> [The Participant–Observer] was supposedly there as a resource. We found that out after she had been on site for months. It had never been explained that she was a counselor; by the time we realized that, we had half of our problems solved. The only time I know of that anyone got any counseling was after the initial test. . . . I hadn't seen [the Project Director] enough to make a difference. By the time I realized [the Principal Investigator] was in Russia, I didn't care.

When structural interventions were attempted, they frequently failed to come as an "integrated socio-technical administrative" package. Although the consultants had, in fact, arranged for key staff to be exposed to a wide range of organizational development techniques, there seemed to be no coherent framework for their adoption. Job enlargement, for example, was sometimes pursued without adequate training, with the result that employees were unable to perform any one job effectively. As one manager put it, "We tried to teach people too much. We had a dozen people doing half a job." Given the nature of Centerton's technology, the attempt to simultaneously master several new jobs and to grapple with a new management style created a learning overload. As one manager stated, "Trying to train everyone in everything should lead a list of "No's" for start-ups." Not surprisingly, when pressed to the wall, most chose to deal with immediate technical problems rather than the ambiguous tasks of participative management.

The consultants later argued that coordination of the Quality of Work Life project suffered because the Personnel Manager, who was expected to take a primary role in implementing the intervention, was unable to accept this responsibility. But it is obvious, in retrospect, that the training he was provided with was simply inadequate for the task. The intervention was sufficiently complex that the consultants (and also the researchers) had difficulty in arriving at correct prescriptions, and it was unrealistic to expect the Personnel Manager—after a relatively brief exposure to Quality of Work Life concepts—to assume such a central role. Thus, effective coordination of the Centerton Quality of Work Life program did not occur and, as a result, the organization was frequently confronted with a potpourri of isolated techniques.

The consequences of this failure to provide an operational "metatheory" of Quality of Work Life principles, are well sum-

marized by Katzel and Yankelovich (1975) in their research
linking work productivity and job satisfaction:

> There exists a wide array of methods available for improving
> workers' job attitudes or performance, but each of them char-
> acteristically tackles some partial aspect of the workers' rela-
> tionship to their jobs. . . . Substantial and enduring improve-
> ments of performance as well as job satisfaction appear to
> require that an integrated combination of methods that relate
> the human to the economic concerns must be employed in order
> to bring about large scale and enduring improvements in both
> domains simultaneously. (p. 13)

From our perspective, this integrated combination was never
achieved in the Centerton Quality of Work Life program.

Credibility of the Consultants. Campbell (1971), in his
description of "the experimenting society," cautions against ad
hominem evaluation:

> The expensive machinery of experimental evaluation should
> only be used where the findings can be generalized to other
> settings and can add to our knowledge of how to manage a good
> society. It should not be wasted on such a petty topic as the
> quality of a specific person. (p. 51)

This is sound advice, and there is little question that any
attempt to assess the personal characteristics of an interventionist is a perilous venture. Yet it is an inescapable fact that
the effectiveness of many social programs rests, to a significant
degree, on more than technical expertise. At Centerton, for
example, the consultants were intended to act as role models
of "auto-critical, not-defensive, openly communicative behavior" (Consultant Progress Report, 1976, p. 31). Thus the skills
needed to successfully implement the intervention could not
be divorced entirely from personal qualities of the change
agents. Because these elements are so important, we will discuss several sensitive issues concerning the consultants that

are not directly related to "technical expertise." The issues which follow are raised in the belief that their omission would leave incomplete the list of intervention problems, and that the experience gained is generalizable to other settings where Quality of Work Life programs might be attempted.

Departure of the Principal Investigator. The loss of the Principal Investigator was a serious blow to the Centerton Quality of Work Life program. Prior to his departure, he had gained the respect and trust of key members of the organization. His popularity was attested to by the fact that in none of the interviews did the evaluators encounter a derogatory comment regarding his performance.

After his departure in May 1974, the responsibility for daily implementation of the intervention shifted to the Participant–Observer. It would be an understatement to suggest that the problem of establishing her role as principal change agent was extraordinarily complex. The respect the Principal Investigator had gained was widespread, and his style was difficult to match. This disadvantage, coupled with the individual focus of many of the Participant–Observer's interventions, led many to discount her expertise. One supervisor commented:

> After the supervisory training, the only intervention was having [the Participant–Observer] around as a consultant. It was nice to have her along to consult; but to call it an intervention? No! To me, [the Principal Investigator] was the authority on participative management—then he was gone. Push it off and come back to see if it was still afloat!

Another supervisor stated bitterly: "We had [the Principal Investigator], who was a fantastic guy, who trained us and left. It might have been different had he been here."

Effectiveness of the Participant–Observer. The Participant–Observer's credibility was further damaged by two unfortunate developments that followed the departure of the Principal Investigator. The first incident occurred during the termination of the Fractionation Manager. This decision was a difficult one, and the Participant–Observer assisted the Plant Manager by helping him clarify his appraisal of the situation and the probable consequences of alternative actions. When the termination decision finally came, however, she became identified with the decision and was subsequently seen by many as an agent of the Plant Manager.

A second event concerned the Participant–Observer's friendship with an outspoken Centerton employee. This relationship provoked strong criticism from some supervisory staff, who felt that the consultant had become a special advocate for a single employee. They complained, for example, that this employee's ideas received inordinate attention—solely because of this association. Under these circumstances, the Participant–Observer was frequently avoided, or otherwise excluded from ongoing plant activities.

It is unfortunate that these events diminished the Participant–Observer's credibility. The task of implementing the Centerton intervention was a complex, stressful job. It was also a job in which she was isolated, since her colleagues were located at some distance. Under these circumstances, it was only natural that strong emotional ties were established with individual members of the organization. The associated liability, however, is that it substantially undermined her credibility as a consultant to the larger organizational system.

Corporate Acquisition. As described in Chapter 4, Crown Medical Specialties was acquired in February 1974 by a foreign multinational organization that had not participated in planning the Quality of Work Life project. The new management took an official position of neutrality, but the consultants argue that this "neutrality" was perceived by some as "subtle sabotage of the program by means of withheld enthusiasm" (Consultant Final Report, 1976, p. 77 ff).

It has long been known that a supportive milieu is essential to the enduring success of organizational change programs (Fleishman, 1953), and the unexpected takeover undoubtedly had an adverse effect on Centerton's Quality of Work Life project. Moreover, the acquisition placed increased financial pressures on the Centerton plant and increased demands for an accelerated start-up operation.

According to the Plant Manager, however, loss of the "protective umbrella," which was to have sheltered the new organization, was not the critical problem:

> [The protective umbrella] wouldn't have helped because when you're participating and not getting started, you will eat people up. Probably what would have happened if we hadn't had the umbrella was that people would have gone away "talking to themselves."

It seems likely that the acquisition may have affected some employees' perceptions of the popularity of the Quality of Work Life project. But interviews with Centerton staff suggest that rejection of the participative philosophy occurred because it was simply not getting results. The program continued in the Quality Assurance Department, and if it had proven successful in other parts of the plant, it seems unlikely that the new management would have responded unfavorably.

Presence of the Evaluators. The presence of a research team undoubtedly complicated the work of the consultants. To an extent, the research increased the time needed for coordination, created some role confusion among Centerton employees, and may have inhibited the consultants' spontaneity in implementing the intervention. Concerning the last point, it is seldom pleasant to have one's professional skills subjected to detailed examination. The change agents generally endured this scrutiny with singular cheerfulness. It seems inevitable, however, that some discomfort was created by the assessment process.

The research had other unintended effects on the intervention. Following the initial selection process, the evaluators submitted an interim report to the funding agency that included an assessment of the new employee program. Because of external deadlines, this report was delivered to the agency with little input from the consultants, and it contained a number of negative findings.

The consultants were understandably irritated at their lack of opportunity for comment, and in addition, disagreed with many substantive findings of the research. This experience suggested that the submission of interim reports might seriously strain the consultant–evaluator relationship and would have the effect of inadvertently placing the evaluators in the role of change agents. Any evaluation is, of course, likely to produce changes in the social system being assessed. But this reactivity may be present in varying degrees. A fundamental premise of the independent evaluation was that the evaluators—to the extent possible—would be free from biases resulting from a vested interest in program outcomes. Thus, it seemed inconsistent to expose the consultants to regular evaluative reports and recommendations which, if implemented, would undermine the basic character of the split-role model. This arrangement would have created the worst of both worlds: a complex researcher–evaluator–client triad lacking the objectivity of independent assessment. It was agreed, therefore, that subsequent reports of the researchers would be of a descriptive—rather than evaluative—nature.

A related problem was discovered only at the conclusion of the study. At this point, the consultants argued that the Institute for Social Research's activities interfered with their own evaluative activity:

> With ISR receiving a grant for evaluation half again larger than (the consultant's) grant for intervention, and with (the consultant's) feeling constricted for funds, we "let ISR do it."

> Had ISR not been in the picture, [we] would have had to take
> periodic soundings and bearings. . . . In that process, we would
> have received written feedback of perceived weakness in the
> intervention sooner than we did and, together with the client
> in our joint venture, promptly would have worked on remedial
> procedures. (Consultant Progress Report, 1976, p. 92)

Our position on the funding issue was that there was no
obviously appropriate ratio of research to intervention expen-
ses. The *raison d'être* of the project was to study the effectiveness of Quality of Work Life concepts in creating new organizations. We felt that each group should be given the funds
needed to perform its role, and—if the consulting budget were
too small—that this was an independent issue to be taken up
with the funding agency. But the consultants' view was understandably different, and it diminished their investment in
self-evaluation.

On the other hand, there were cases in which the Institute
for Social Research data seemed to be useful. For example, a
Quality Assurance Supervisor commented:

> I find myself going back quite a bit and doing extra things that
> didn't get done just because of the ISR. And I'd like the point
> made that I think the ISR questionnaire has been more of a
> help to my management than the training . . . back in October.

Since the evaluators were attempting to play an unobtrusive role, having had an impact on the Quality of Work Life
program is not necessarily to their credit. Nevertheless, in the
Quality Assurance Department where the Quality of Work
Life program was most effective, the presence of the evaluators
had some beneficial results; thus the "reactivity" of the assessment seems to have had both positive and negative consequences.

Conclusion. It is possible to sort problems with the Centerton Quality of Work Life program into three general cate-

gories: difficulties of initial conceptualization, problems in program implementation, and "exogenous shocks"—unforeseen external events which exacerbated the effects of the first two. The consultants later contended that these outside forces were, by far, the most damaging. The Principal Investigator argued, for example, that

> The catastrophic changes brought about by the new corporate management's attitude and the stresses and strains at start-up simply made it too difficult for managers and supervisors to take advantage of what was offered. After November 1974, the climate for growth and change was simply not there!

No calculus exists for weighting the relative importance of problems that were encountered. From the evaluators' perspective, however, it appears that difficulties in conceptualization and implementation were more damaging than external forces. It is interesting to note that this divergence of opinion might have been anticipated by a perceptive attribution theorist: Actors tend to attribute failures to environmental forces, whereas observers tend to base causal explanations on the characteristics of the actors (Jones & Nisbett, 1972).

The possibility of "attribution error" (Bierbrauer, 1973) exists, but there is also reason to believe that serious conceptual and practical problems existed independently of these external events. Much of this has already been considered, and will not be repeated here. In general, however, the environmental explanation is not supported by (1) evidence that serious misunderstandings about the consultants' concepts and ideology were encountered in the Quality Assurance Department, which was relatively insulated from corporate pressures; (2) the finding that the Quality Assurance Department, which consistently attempted to implement intervention principles, generally followed the same developmental path as the Production Department, which did not; and (3) the conviction of Centerton managers that the program was producing serious problems that would not have been eliminated by a "protective umbrella." Although not discounting the adverse impact of environmental forces, we are led by this consistent pattern of results to believe that significant problems of conceptualization and implementation would have remained—even had the Centerton program been initiated in a more hospitable environment.

Generic Problems in Creating High Involvement Organizations

A series of predictable problems surface in high involvement plant start-ups. Some of these problems can be anticipated and solved or prevented; others are more difficult to deal with. A quick review of these general problems and their potential solutions will highlight what we have learned about starting high involvement plants from our work at Centerton and our visits to other new plants.

Unrealistic Expectations. The innovative selection process that has been used in many of the new Quality of Work Life plants often combines with the initial enthusiasm of the managers to create very high expectations on the part of the work force. Because of the stress the selection interviews place on challenging work and autonomy, employees often expect that things will be "totally" different. They develop expectations about always having interesting work to do and being able to control their own work life. In some instances, such as Centerton, these expectations were not met and serious problems resulted.

At Centerton, many employees felt a sense of betrayal when situational demands led to a reassessment of the Quality of Work Life program and a curtailment of unbounded participation. To compound the problem, when those in supervisory positions began to exercise their formal authority, many seemed to experience a sense of guilt that they had failed to live up to the consultants' Quality of Work Life philosophy.

At Centerton as well as at other plants in which expectations have not been met, workers have either quit or stayed on and complained about the difference between what they anticipated work to be like and how it actually turned out. The irony here is that, in many of the cases where unrealistic expectations have been a problem, the work situations offered more autonomy and interesting work than typically exists; unfortunately, this fact is offset by failure to meet employees' expectations. The solution would appear to be to work toward more realistic expectations on the part of employees, but this is not always easy to do in a new plant situation. Often management doesn't really know what will evolve, and there is no ongoing work for "future" employees to observe.

Individual Differences. People differ in their needs, skills, abilities, values, and preferences. A great deal of research has shown that not all individuals respond positively to the kinds of innovations tried in high involvement plants. Some simply prefer the more traditional ways of doing things, and the selection process cannot screen out all of those individuals who do not belong in a participative environment.

Our study of Centerton suggests that the group interview may have serious deficiencies as a selection device and, what is more, it may even be discriminatory. The failure of the group approach is not surprising, since group interviews are not known for their validity. But we strongly recommend that new, high involvement plants look to additional selection devices. If they decide to use the interview approach, then it is imperative that the selectors be trained to do structured interviews and to avoid discriminatory hiring decisions.

Even if more effective selection procedures are used, however, new plants must be prepared to work with individuals who do not fit into a high involvement work situation. Unfortunately, there are no easy prescriptions for dealing with these individuals. Many quit, but others stay and continue to resist quality of work life activities. In most plants visited, some individuals—usually those who didn't participate in team meetings—finally had to be fired because they prevented the teams from functioning effectively. This is an extreme solution, and strategies need to be developed for using the talents of those who have difficulty adapting to the demands of the organization.

Role of First Level Supervision. Probably the most frequent, and most serious, problem in the high involvement plant involves the role of the first level supervisor. A number of different approaches have been taken to the dilemmas associated with this role. To some extent, the strategy depends on the individuals occupying supervisory positions. In some cases, relatively traditional foremen are in place; in others, there is no first level supervisor present and it is assumed that the groups will be self-managing. In still other situations, individuals have been put in as acting first level supervisors and told to work themselves out of their job within a year or so of start-up.

Regardless of the approach, however, problems have appeared. In almost all instances with which we are familiar, those individuals who are in the first level supervisory positions complain of a lack of role clarity, confusion about the decisions they can and cannot make, and a great deal of ambiguity about their power and responsibility. As was true at Centerton, they are uncomfortable with directing people to do things because they feel things should be done participatively. But in many cases supervisors simply don't know how to make participation operational. They often lack the skills to help the group function as a team, make decisions, and work through issues. They also have a great deal of difficulty deciding which decisions should be made on a participative basis and which should not. For example, at Centerton, supervisors sought out participation on issues for which they already possessed all the information and technical expertise necessary to make a decision. This caused frustrating delays; it was both inefficient and time consuming.

Perhaps the best way to point out what is lacking here is to state that no clearcut description of the first level supervisor's responsibilities exists. Because of this, there are no adequate training or selection programs for somebody striving to fill this position. Training ends up being hit-or-miss business, and the failure rate for those selected is often high. Several organizations are developing training programs to address the problem, but their effectiveness has yet to be established. Thus, we have no clear recommendation on how to deal with this problem other than to stress the importance of providing supervisors with concrete models to guide them in establishing a clear identity in the organizational role structure.

Permissiveness versus Participation. One of the hardest issues for managers in new Quality of Work Life plants concerns the difference between permissiveness and participation. In most new high involvement plants, employees have raised issues that seemed to the managers to go "too far." For example, at Centerton, the workers wanted to install a color television set in a work area. The managers considered this undesirable, but had a great deal of difficulty responding because they felt if they denied the request they would violate the participative spirit of the plant. They finally refused, however, in the belief that a positive response would harm productivity and represent an example of permissiveness rather than participative management.

The problem experienced by this group of managers is typical of what has occurred in other plants when workers have requested unusual personnel rules or work procedures. Unfortunately, what represents a reasonable or unreasonable request is often unclear. There is probably little way to deal with this kind of issue in advance, but it is evident that the method by which such issues are dealt with can greatly influence the future of the plant. Arbitrary dismissal of a request can destroy the participative spirit of the plant, just as acceptance of every suggestion for eliminating rules, regulations, and discipline can create havoc. One recommendation for dealing with this problem is the creation of a representative "microcosm" group from various functions and levels of the organization. These decision-making groups can help formalize the company's commitment to participation and, at the same time, make workplace decisions in a fair and reasonable way.

Office Area. As was true at Centerton, most plants seem to have trouble conceiving of new ways to treat office and clerical employees. As a result, these employees often feel unappreciated. They can end up doing exactly the same jobs they would have had in a more traditional plant and, although they may be supervised in a more participative manner, their life isn't that different—even though they are often told that they are in a "Quality of Work Life" or participative organization. What is needed here, of course, are innovative approaches to organizing, training, and paying office workers. Some creative designs have been used successfully, such as rotating employees between shipping and office jobs, but more emphasis needs to be placed on these positions.

Personnel Function. The personnel function is usually much more important in new design plants and requires a very different set of skills than those held by a traditional personnel manager. Since many conventional personnel tasks are allocated to the work teams, many of the activities that personnel managers typically engage in (e.g., pay administration, selection) are partially absent from the job. However, the Personnel Manager must still act as a key resource, using interpersonal skills to work with the line organizations in implementing the management philosophy of the plant. In many cases, the Personnel Manager ends up having a very difficult and at times frustrating job. In some cases, the Personnel Manager is asked for solutions to problems that have never been tackled before. The only recommendation that can be made here is to stress the importance of carefully selecting a talented, flexible individual, and providing him or her with the training and support needed to perform this unique role. Because Centerton never fully understood the requirements of the position, a person with traditional skills was hired. Thus he was never able to perform his job in accordance with the Quality of Work Life approach.

Regression Under Pressure. At some point in the history of most new plant start-ups, whether a high involvement type or not, a period of intense pressure for production usually develops. The pressure stems from the need to get the on line plant functioning in accordance with a predetermined production schedule. This has proved to be a particularly crucial period in the life of most new Quality of Work Life plants. Most managers tend to revert to traditional management practices when things become difficult, reacting to crises by attempting to take charge; managers reacted this way several times at Centerton. Needless to say, such actions can be very damaging to a successful start-up because they communicate to everyone that the new principles of management are only applicable when things are going well. Although most new Quality of Work Life plants have successfully maintained their commitment to participative management during this period, there are exceptions. We recommend that a strong commitment at all levels of the organization be established before a new design plant is started. If this commitment is lacking, then the effort should probably not be undertaken at all.

Timing of Start-Up Activities. At the present time, no clear road map exists to provide guidance for scheduling the start-up activities of a Quality of Work Life plant. Each organization must wrestle with questions like these: When should the pay system be developed? When are personnel policies to be set? When should the first employee be hired? When should groups be established?

The answers to these questions are crucial since they influence the success of any effort. In some cases, timing may be as important as content. For example, the nature of the technology and the skills of the employees must both be considered when an implementation schedule is drawn up. The experience at Centerton suggests that the newer and more complex the technology, the more slowly the "new management practices" should be put into effect. If everything is put into play at once, there is simply too much to learn. When the plant requires introduction of a changing or complex technology, it may be best to institute an intermediate organizational design and abandon it once the technology has been mastered by the employees.

Some projects may have gotten into trouble because "the final organization design" was embraced prematurely. For example, autonomous work groups have sometimes been formed at the start-up of production even though the technology did not allow for stable group membership at that time. A successful effort requires both a carefully articulated plan for continual training in participative management and an implementation plan that covers such issues as job enrichment and new pay approaches.

Relations with the Rest of the Organization. In one sense, high involvement plants are foreign bodies inside larger organizations. They differ in a number of important ways from the organizations that created them, and to which they are responsible. In every new plant we are aware of (whether successful or not) this discrepancy created a number of "interface" problems; these problems have received the most public attention in the case of the Topeka dog food plant. At

Topeka, some plant level managers came into conflict with line and staff managers at the corporate level and ultimately left the corporation.

The generic interface problem illustrated by Topeka results from the threat new plants pose to the traditional organization. As living demonstrations that there is a different way to do things, they pose a difficult question: Does the rest of the organization need to change? Managers on the corporate staff may be threatened because they are accustomed to dealing with issues in a standardized way. If demands begin to arise from other parts of the organization for a more individualized response, these managers may feel that their inability to change will cost them their jobs. Because new design plants operate with fewer managers, some line managers may question their own job security. In addition, managers in other plants may be concerned that they will have to change their whole approach to management if the new plants succeed. Finally, managers may feel their upward mobility in the organization will be hampered by successful managers in the new plants.

No organization has yet solved the interface issue, but some are trying interesting approaches. The most successful approaches emphasize decentralization and communication, stressing both that differences are acceptable and that open communication can defuse anxiety. Communications devices have included seminars, task forces to study and design new plants, and frequent visits to new plants by outsiders.

Implications for a High Involvement Model. Centerton tried some approaches to organization and management that we found to be characteristic of other high involvement plants. They followed a similar approach to selection, management style, the physical design of the plant, and training. They also made some effort to redesign jobs; however, as we noted in Chapter 7, Centerton can best be described as a partially developed Quality of Work Life plant. Significant adoption of participative management practices took place only in the Quality Assurance Department and, even there, many things had to be handled in a traditional manner. This occurred because of the failure of the rest of the system to adopt a Quality of Work Life approach, and because the quality of work life approach actually adopted excluded a number of potential design elements.

Because utilization of the components of the model was limited, the Centerton experience can tell us very little about the model's potential. A true test of the potential of high involvement organizations can only be accomplished by studying situations in which most or all of the key practices are implemented. A startling success at Centerton would have raised serious questions about the need for many design components and the systemic nature of organizational design and change. If Centerton had fully succeeded, it would have been a counterexample to the view that organizations must be internally consistent and systemic to be highly effective. In fact, Centerton seemed to perform just as might have been predicted: moderately well.

The Centerton case indicates that adoption of the high involvement mode of operation should not be taken lightly. Effective implementation demands a large prestart-up commitment on the part of the organization as well as continuing, long-term support. A considerable amount of prestart-up planning and study will be needed, with consulting assistance in specialized areas. At this point, many personnel managers lack the experience necessary to put together a new Quality of Work Life plant. Because total system change is involved, help will be needed from individuals who are broadly knowledgeable and who can maintain effective interpersonal relationships. In addition, a number of situational factors must be favorable for the high involvement model to be successfully implemented. Key among these are compatible technology and strong, unwavering corporate support.

Chapter Ten

Managing Creation: Meeting the Developmental Needs of New Organizations

This chapter outlines those elements of the Centerton experience that appear to have special relevance for other new settings, including the special case of new organizations using advanced technology. Our discussion is comprised of three major sections. First, we will review the history of the Centerton start-up and reexamine the role of our theoretical model as a tool for understanding the developmental properties of new organizations. Second, we will explore the issue of causal relationships, describing a series of analyses intended to trace the emergent forces that were operating in the early days of the Centerton life cycle. Finally, we move to a discussion of intervention strategies implied by the special characteristics of new organizations.

STAGES, BOUNDARIES, SCHEMAS, AND ERAS

The pattern of events we observed at Centerton conforms, with considerable fidelity, to the theoretical schema proposed in Chapter 2. There were some deviations, but the essential structure fit quite well. The initial days were characterized by inordinately high expectations; these hopes were battered by the emotional and technical problems associated with start-up; and a painful reexamination occurred with the November Kiem-Tau. Predictable power struggles ensued, resulting in the termination of one key figure in the organizational hierarchy and an ensuing period of consolidation. Then, consistent with theoretical prediction, the organization was riven by interpersonal conflict before arriving at a stable period of productive equilibrium.

The Centerton saga thus provides support for our theory of organizational creation, but it wouuld undoubtedly be a mistake to dogmatically apply our template to the events characterizing the organization's beginning. To be sure, there were stages and discontinuities in the process of growth. But it is also important to recognize the continuities: Each era in the life cycle was inextricably linked to its successor and predecessor. As Sarason (1972) puts it:

> the belief that there are stages or phases which are distinct, bounded, and real . . . is akin to the reaction we frequently have when we drive past a road sign telling us we are now in a different state. Somehow the sign makes us feel real change at the same time we are aware that our feeling is not justified. There is, of course, some external basis to the concept of phases or stages—just as the highway sign signifies a real political–legal change—but one must be very careful not to over-emphasize discontinuity and to under-emphasize continuity. (p. 68)

One is reminded of the apocryphal story of a Vermont farmer who, because of a shift in the river bounding his property, became a citizen of the state of New Hampshire. "Thank God," he remarked, "I couldn't have stood another of those Vermont winters." Sometimes the transitional periods in the creation of an organization may be equally subtle. But at some point it becomes clear that one is, indeed, in another temporal region; the terrain has changed, and the managerial challenges have been altered.

A second point to be made is that passage through a particular period does not necessarily imply that resolution has been complete. Just as the tasks of individual development can reemerge in Erikson's epigenetic matrix, organizational problems can return if they have been only partially confronted— or if new actors arrive who have not experienced the process of creation.

Perhaps a developmental stage is most accurately portrayed as a period in which a unique creational issue is prepotent. But other concerns may intrude to a greater or lesser extent, and a crucial task may even be suppressed. Thus the distinctiveness of developmental stages will vary across situations, influenced by environmental forces and individual differences in the composition of key players.

Centerton, for example, operated in a unique market environment. As a high level Crown manager observed, manufacturing a product that is injected directly into human beings is a different task than manufacturing pet food. This has obvious implications for quality control, and the importance attached to that function was reflected in the Centerton organization structure: The Quality Assurance Manager was insulated from conflict with the Plant Manager by his corporate reporting relationship. In addition, it was significant that the Quality Assurance Manager was more interested in product integrity than in organizational politics. In McCleland's (1961) terms, his goals were more directed toward achievement than toward power and influence.

The effect of these conditions was that the principal leadership challenge came from a young, flamboyant Production Manager who reported directly to the Plant Manager. Had no such person existed, it is conceivable that the resolution of leadership would have taken longer—perhaps played out in a series of skirmishes between the Quality Assurance manager and the Plant Manager—and blurring the lines of demarcation in the Centerton saga.

TRACING CAUSALITY: CRITICAL FORCES IN THE CENTERTON START-UP

In a series of analyses reported elsewhere (Perkins, Nieva, & Lawler, 1978), we investigated causal relationships among a number of key measures using the method of cross-lagged panel correlation described in Chapter 6. The results of these analyses were intriguing. During the period from November 1974 to December 1975, many causal relationships were the reverse of those we expected to find. Three of four hypothesized "outcome" measures actually appeared to "produce" effects on characteristics of the organization that we had regarded as independent variables. We initially hypothesized, for example, that increased involvement would result from Centerton's success in improving the quality of working life for its employees. But we were surprised to find that the degree of employee involvement actually seemed to determine the way they perceived the quality of life in the organization. For example, those who were highly involved during the first measurement period also saw their work groups as cohesive and their pay as equitable.

In later stages of development, however, this relationship did not hold; in the second measurement period, from December 1975 to January 1977, the pattern reversed itself. The predicted pattern of relationships emerged quite clearly, and involvement was then influenced by five of the predicted "intervening" variables: group fragmentation; conflict resolution by fate control; pay equity; and organizational trust.

Deviations from commonly held conceptions of causality are not unknown in organizational research (see Lowin & Craig,

1968), but these patterns have special significance in new organizations. Since the so-called outcome variables seem to be immune to influence by the hypothesized "causal" variables, it is not easy to see how they can be affected by factors under the control of managers or change agents. In our example, it is relatively easy to see how equitable pay and a positive team climate might contribute to employee involvement. But how can employee involvement be enhanced if, in the utopian period, involvement itself is the source of employee attitudes about the organization?

Questions also arise concerning the nature of this causal shift. We wondered, for example, whether our outcome variables actually exchanged roles by producing changes in intervening variables that would be corroborated by other measures. Since our observational data have not been quantified, this issue cannot be examined using formal techniques for causal modeling. In some cases, however, it seems likely that a direct causal shift may have occurred. It is quite reasonable to believe, for example, that greater work satisfaction—an outcome measure—led to decreases in perceived role overload. Similarly, greater employee involvement may well have led to decreased work group fragmentation.

On the other hand, it seems less likely that, as our self-report data suggest, greater work satisfaction produced more effective supervisory work facilitation. Or that increased involvement had direct effects on pay equity—measured by some independent means. It is not impossible that these processes occurred, of course, but it seems more likely that a large portion of the observed effects were simply a function of the altered perceptions of setting members. To illustrate, satisfied individuals would be more apt to view their supervisors as facilitating than would disgruntled employees. And highly involved members would understandably feel that they were receiving an equitable paycheck, while alienated or indifferent individuals could be expected to express dissatisfaction with their compensation.

Later in the organizational life cycle we did not see these paradoxical patterns. At this point, our results suggest that the outcome measures were, in fact, influenced by the hypothesized causal variables. In only one case did the reverse influence process appear: Employee satisfaction seemed to produce effects on employees' higher order needs. Again, two explanations are possible. Either individuals who were satisfied with their work tended to find jobs that satisfied their needs for growth, or satisfied employees simply perceived their jobs as more varied, autonomous, and so forth. Lacking objective measures of task characteristics—such as the job observation schema proposed by Jenkins, Nadler, Lawler, and Cammann (1975)—these two alternatives cannot be completely untangled. However, since there were few objective changes in jobs or staff assignments, it appears highly likely that the effects were largely a result of shifts in individual perceptions.

The perceptual differences between the two phases are consistent with our theory of emergent social systems, which suggests that organizational growth resembles the development of smaller settings. This isomorphism permits us to view the utopian period of an organization alongside what may be a more familiar scene of social creation: the "honeymoon" stage of marriage. Sarason (1972) has observed that

> the creation of settings . . . provisionally may be defined as any instance in which two or more people come together in a new relationship over a sustained period of time in order to achieve certain goals. The most frequent instance is, of course, when two people enter into marriage. The most ambitious instance would be when people band together for the express purpose of creating a new society. (pp. 1–2)

There are those who would question whether creating a successful new marriage is any less ambitious a task than launching a new society. But the examples are nevertheless instructive, since they underscore the common set of characteristics shared by many "new settings."

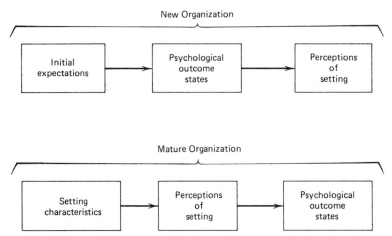

Figure 10-1   Causal relationships in new and mature organizations.

One such feature is clearly the initial expectations and perceptions with which people enter a new relationship. Whether this relationship is a marital arrangement or a new presidential administration, their inaugurations are usually characterized by an intransigent set of initial attitudes. And the use of the phrase "honeymoon period" to describe both new marriages and new administrations is not accidental: As we have argued, the psychological processes in each case are quite similar.

Whether one voted for or against a particular candidate, the attitudes that influenced this behavior are not easily altered—at least not during the early days of office. Over time, however, initial perceptions may shift in correspondence with observed behavior—admittedly, more so for some voters than for others.

As shown in Figure 10-1, this process is one in which an initial perceptual orientation produces a set of psychological states which, in turn, color individual perceptions of the setting. As social systems mature, however, the realities of relationships emerge. Narcissistic marriage partners are seen as such, scurrilous politicians have their tapes subpoenaed, and organizations are seen for what they really are. By this point, only the most inflexible are able to cling to their initial, contradictory beliefs.

In addition to this perceptual twist, one other finding from our causal analysis deserves mention. In examining relationships among outcome variables, we found that work satisfaction initially "produced" effects on employees' life satisfaction. Later, however, no relationship was found.

This result is supported by our clinical observation of Centerton's developmental history. In the beginning of the start-up effort, most of those engaged in building the new organization were consumed with the task. Personal satisfactions were largely derived from experiences in the workplace, and every waking hour was devoted to getting the production process started. Later, however, the climate changed.

As the months passed, many initial obstacles were overcome and employees spent a much smaller portion of their lives struggling to build the new organization. And as time wore on, many among the core group suffered from a sense of "burnout." For these individuals, the intense effort which had been expended in the beginning could not be sustained, and they were forced to differentiate between personal and professional roles.

For other employees, the decreasing relationship between work and life satisfaction resulted from changes in the character of the maturing organization. For the entrepreneurs who thrived on the excitement and challenge of creation, the improved functioning of the organization may have had the effect of decreasing their enjoyment of the job. As initial problems were overcome and routines were established, these "initiators" simply lost interest in the task.

The perceptual changes that attend organizational creation make it clear that intervening in a new work setting is not a simple task. But the Centerton experience and our theory of creation point to a number of strategies for improving the start-up process; these points of leverage will be discussed next.

INTERVENTION STRATEGIES

The strategies described here are of two basic sorts. First, there are those techniques and perspectives that are relevant throughout the beginning stages of creation. Their applicability extends from utopianism to equilibrium. Second, there are interventions that are particularly appropriate at critical junctures within a specific period of growth. We will begin by discussing more general intervention issues, and then move to a set of recommendations more directly linked to the developmental state of the organization.

Managing Boundaries: The Challenge of Matching Organizational States and Stages

Perhaps the first point to be made is that new organizations are significantly different from mature ones. Our theory of creation underscores the fact that new organizations are characterized by constant change, and our empirical data document concomitant effects on individual perceptions.

Since these features now appear obvious, it may seem unnecessary to place so much weight on the uniqueness of new social settings. But Centerton's special characteristics were not nearly so apparent to us or the consultants in the beginning. Since others may be similarly misled, it is important to emphasize the fact that techniques that have proven successful in mature settings may be inadequate when applied to the special problems of new organizations. In these settings, attempts to employ "traditional" methods may well end in frustration.

There is evidence that this error may be a common one, and Alderfer and Berg's (1977) conceptualization is helpful in explaining why. They argue that interventionists often fail to distinguish between "underbounded" and "overbounded" systems. In contrast to mature, overbounded settings, the typical situation to be confronted in an underbounded organization is one of unclear authority structure, uncertain role definitions, and confused communication patterns.

This description paints a nearly stereotypic picture of the new organization. In the beginning of its life cycle, a new setting cannot help suffering from the ambiguity that exists when internal structures have yet to be created. Thus a key managerial task is one of moving the organization away from this underbounded condition; intervention activities should facilitate this process.

Unfortunately, many of the most popular interventions were developed in mature, bureaucratic organizations afflicted by a set of problems quite different from those characteristic of new settings. Consequently, the blind application of these techniques can exacerbate rather than alleviate organizational problems. As Alderfer (1979) notes:

> Within the organization development literature, there is a growing list of "failures," which may be understood, in part, as the result of applying interventions designed for overbounded systems to underbounded problems. (p. 271)

From this perspective, it is clear why the concept of participative management introduced at Centerton created such severe problems. In a setting with ill-defined authority relationships and managers afraid to set limits, a decision making structure that many interpreted as "one person, one vote" had the effect of exaggerating the lack of internal boundaries.

The essential managerial task in a new organization is to create a set of system characteristics—authority relations, role definitions, and so forth—which are congruent with each stage of the organizational life cycle. At the inception of a new organization, this means creating boundaries where none previously existed. As the organization matures, however, these structures will evolve and the organization must be continually adjusted to maintain an optimal degree of system boundedness.

Managing Stress: Coping with the Strains of Creation

The beginning of organizational life is laden with elements that create stress in other social settings. From our theory of creation it is apparent that change is inevitable as new organizations negotiate one developmental crisis after another. The strains associated with change have been well documented, as have the repercussions of interpersonal conflict (see Holmes & Rahe, 1967). A new organization is affected by both these stressors as well as by other factors.

Conditions that have been found to produce emotional and physical strain in mature organizations (see Kahn, 1973) are magnified in new settings. Role overload, for example, seems to be a predictable feature of the start-up process. Long working hours and impossible deadlines are the rule rather than the exception. Ambiguity is another concomitant of creation. In a struggling, underbounded system, roles are evolving rather than established; the confusion that accompanies this process can be debilitating. Role conflicts are also common, since the demands of creation often result in simultaneous, antagonistic demands for employees' time.

Because the combined effects of these conditions can be overwhelming, stress management is a critical issue in new organizations. Qualitative overload, which occurs when individuals are taxed beyond their abilities, can be controlled in part by careful selection. At Centerton, considerable effort went into the design of the selection process; but the lack of emphasis on technical knowledge meant that inexperienced employees were often subjected to an excruciating learning overload. In addition, later opportunities to compensate for these skill deficits were lost when start-up delays were used for cleaning and maintenance rather than for technical instruction.

If a well-designed training program had been introduced instead, perhaps later role overload would have been reduced. Of course, this opportunity is clearer in hindsight than it was at the time, and a technical training package was unavailable. But the lesson suggests one way in which advance preparation can be used to help capitalize on these unexpected—yet probably unavoidable—delays.

Problems with quantitative overload—that is, having too much work to accomplish—can be eased simply by relaxing deadlines. This is often easier said than done, of course, since the intensity of organizational growth generates a compelling sense of urgency. But experience suggests that rigid deadlines may work in the short run at the expense of long term organizational effectiveness: At some point, employees may simply "burn out" as a result of unrealistic demands.

The burnout problem may be minimized by other techniques, such as the use of organizational designs that conserve human resources. The Plant Manager, for example, later suggested that

> the start-up group and the operating group should be two different teams. Because of the stresses and strains of start-up, the work could better be done by a group that's temporarily located there. . . . They're available at all hours, they expect it, and that's what they get. When they get their job done, they pack up and go home.

This strategy has been adopted by the military in amphibious assaults, where specially trained landing teams are assigned the role of securing beachheads for regular infantry units. And those who have participated in the creation of new organizations usually have no difficulty seeing the connection between an organizational start-up and a military campaign.

This "baton passing" model is not without disadvantages—in particular, the risk that diffusion of responsibility will cause problems in transition. To improve continuity, a nucleus of start-up staff can be designated to remain with the organization into the period of steady state. This variation provides a sense of institutional memory, so the thinking that went into the planning process will be retained. It also creates an awareness of the need for workable, enduring structures.

There are also reasons to select members of the creation team who are aware of the special needs of those who will follow. During the Centerton start-up, the design of the physical structure was executed entirely by males. One result was that the dressing facilities for female operators opened directly onto the break room, from which the shower was fully visible. It seems unlikely that this oversight would have occurred had women been involved in the planning process. Of course, the baton passing model is inherently vulnerable to such problems; but if care is taken to deal with transitional issues, a two-team approach can help to minimize the stresses associated with start-up.

Finally, there is reason to believe that the effects of "creational stress" can be mitigated by encouraging the development of supportive interpersonal relationships. Building positive relationships is, of course, a ubiquitous human relations prescription. But a supportive organizational climate has been found to buffer the frictions of role ambiguity, role overload, and physiological strain (French, 1973; House & Wells, 1978)—all of which are predictable features of new organizations. This implies that it is particularly important for the creators of new organizations to establish a climate in which social support systems can develop. For example, time can be set aside for employees to share the stresses that they are experiencing, engage in mutual problem solving around coping strategies, and maintain a sense of cohesiveness and common purpose.

Paradise Lost: Dealing with Utopianism

Our causal analyses and clinical observations support the belief that individual attitudes are relatively immune to influence during the initial honeymoon period. Consequently, those who enter the organization with high expectations are likely to maintain them until the objective properties of the environment take hold. There is also reason to believe that these attitudes can be influenced by the nature of the selection process. Both consistency theory (Festinger, 1957) and attribution theory (Bem, 1967) would suggest that individuals who enter new organizations with high expectations will, at least initially, exhibit correspondingly high levels of satisfaction and involvement. And there is also evidence that these expectations can be manipulated through the design of selection procedures—for example, the arduous initiation conducted by Aronson and Mills (1959)—or through bombastic recruiting rhetoric.

There are, however, a number of reasons why attempts to improve these attitudes by inflating expectations is a bad idea. To begin with, practicing cosmetic surgery on an organizational image is as unethical as it is pervasive. And even if this strategem is successful in attracting desirable job candidates, there is evidence that distorted perceptions can create serious problems as these individuals begin to experience organizational reality (Porter, Lawler, & Hackman, 1975). This was certainly true at Centerton. The Plant Manager later commented:

> I think our preparation and training . . . presented the idea that there was going to be one big, happy family here where every-

one was competent, and everyone was going to do their job and
the family circle was going to stay intact. . . . There weren't
going to be any disappointments. And then we got into it and
found that people are really human after all.

To counter such problems, Wanous (1975, 1977) argues for
the use of "realistic job previews." This strategy replaces the
typical panoply of unrealistic promises with a balanced pres-
entation of accurate, detailed information about the work environment as it really is.

It might at first appear that this sort of candor would make
it difficult, if not impossible, to recruit new employees. In the
majority of studies in which realistic previews were tested,
however, no adverse effects were found. And it seems likely
that those who selected themselves out because of accurate
advance information would have eventually done so anyway:
In all of the "realistic preview" cases cited by Wanous (1977),
the survival rate for the control group was lower than for those
whose jobs were portrayed truthfully.

Wanous' findings are consistent with other research. Janis
and Mann (1977), for example, found that surgery patients
were better able to deal with adversity when prepared in advance for possible mishaps. This process has also proven beneficial in work settings, when individuals have been given
"stress inoculation" prior to retiring or taking a new job (Janis
& Wheeler, 1978).

The convergence of these independent research themes can
be explained by work on causal attribution and personal control. The need to move efficaciously through a consistent, manageable world is a persistent finding in psychological research
(see de Charms, 1968; Festinger, 1957; White, 1959). People
apparently try to master their environments or—failing that—
reconstruct reality in an effort to regain the illusion of control.
The effect of this need for control is that people understate the
effects of chance events; they deny the importance of outside

forces; and they make specious connections between their behavior and "uncontrollable" life events (Wortman, 1976).

All this implies that an accurate awareness of the developmental problems of new organizations is acutely important. First, potential employees who are badly matched will have the opportunity to "opt out" before they and the organization have expended needless time and energy in the adjustment process. Second, those who do join will be better able to cope. Understanding the probable developmental scenario may, for example, allow individuals to come to grips with the fact that there may be events over which they have relatively little control. This awareness can prevent disabling feelings of "learned helplessness" (Seligman, 1975) by helping employees judge when they can and cannot intervene to control their work environment.

Psychological inoculation of new members can begin at the time of recruitment and continue throughout the organization's early stages of growth. As part of the selection design, for example, promising job candidates can be introduced to the demands of start-up through accounts of individuals who have already experienced the process. The characteristics of creation can also be introduced using theoretical material of the sort we have presented. A conceptual framework can help individuals to understand the sources of turbulence they will encounter and will help them to organize their own experiences.

Participants might also be encouraged to share experiences they have had in the creation of other "new settings." Although some individuals may be involved for the first time in the birth of a new organization, our conceptualization suggests that experiences in other social systems may be valuable. Encounters with small groups, or even new relationships, could be used to help identify likely future scenarios and develop contingency plans to counter probable trouble spots.

Conflict, Challenge, and Confrontation

As illustrated in the previous discussion of stages and schemas, the predicted challenge to authority may be influenced by a number of individual and situational variables. For example, the intensity of conflict experienced in this phase can be significantly altered by a leader's managerial style. It is difficult to savagely attack a charismatic leader whose expert powers are incontrovertible, but an inept tyrant may experience the full force of group rebellion.

It is interesting to note that, although there are advantages to moderating the intensity of conflict, delaying its onset may have considerable costs. Slater (1966) argues that:

> In the case of the attack on the group leader . . . the earlier the attack comes in the history of the group the more satisfying it seems to be. Revolts occurring early in the group's history are permanently treasured as events inaugurating group strength and group life. Those taking place at mid-passage impart a feeling of group solidity along with a kind of disillusionment—a feeling that the revolt did not make as much difference as anticipated. Those that occur near the end are generally felt to have been sterile exercises or self-conscious rituals, despite the fact that the later the revolt the more considered, significant, and truly experimental it is in prospect. (p. 79)

There is also evidence that leader–member conflicts can be moderated by structural mechanisms. For example, Goldenberg (1971) describes the effects of a transitional leadership design on the Residential Youth Center. The first Director of this organization had defined his role as a time-limited one, both because of the stresses of start-up and because of the values of the institution:

> In many ways, the fate of the RYC might have been very different had not its first leader had "somewhere to go" (i.e.,

back to the university) after completing his six months as Director. It is more than likely that had he remained as the RYC's Director, he would have done little to help the setting in terms of its continuing development. He was, as his final diary indicates, "used up and finished," and had he been "forced" either by personal or "system-wide" considerations to perpetuate his tenure of office, it is quite conceivable that neither he nor the program would have benefitted from this prolongation of "tour of duty." (Goldenberg, 1971, pp. 324–325)

This transitional structure thus enabled the Director to recover from the stresses of creation. But it may also have had the effect of blunting challenges to his authority, since some staff members would be likely to await the arrival of the new Director before negotiating power relationships.

This possibility has important implications for a baton-passing model of start-up. If the negotiation of power relationships is, as Slater suggests, an essential developmental task, then an organizational design that sidesteps confrontation may leave important emotional issues unresolved. In fact, we might speculate that the intensity of intergroup conflict later experienced at the RYC might have had its origins in this transitional design; that is, it may have been exaggerated by displaced leader–member confrontation.

This is speculative, of course, and further study of the effects of alternative leadership designs is badly needed. But it is clear that leadership in a new organization is indeed a complex affair. There is evidence to suggest that leader–member conflict is a concomitant of creation, and that issues of power should be confronted early on. At the same time, there are ways of mitigating the negative outcomes of such clashes. For example, a leadership style that encourages the direct expression of opinion will help prevent pent-up aggression from exploding in an uncontrolled outburst.

Third party intervention can also be employed; it is a strategy that has been used in conflict situations extending from divorce settlements to international disputes. At Centerton, the Participant–Observer's perceived lack of impartiality made it difficult for her to facilitate the resolution of conflict between the Plant Manager and his Fractionation Manager. But Walton (1969) has demonstrated that third-party consultants can be effective. They can, for example, help maintain the motivation of participants engaged in the process of conflict resolution. Third-party facilitators can also serve as a counterweight to equalize situational power imbalances; and they can use their process skills to provide social support, encourage openness, and maintain optimum tension levels between protagonists.

This role is one that requires considerable skill, since the interventionist must turn antagonism into problem solving (Filley, 1975) by creating a climate of trust and acceptance. This is no easy task in an organizational start-up. Nevertheless, examples of successful third-party intervention do exist (see Walton, 1969), and effective conflict resolution is critical in this period of organizational growth.

Following the period of leader–member conflict, a setting that conforms to our theoretical scenario will enter a period of resolution. Those who have been buffeted by the trials of earlier growth stages may find some relief in a brief respite. At this point in the development of a new organization, many of the vexatious early problems will have been resolved. Most employees will have offices, filing cabinets, desks, tools, or whatever personal equipment they need to do their jobs. The new machinery (that was promised to be flawlessly engineered and delivered in perfect condition) will finally be running, or the service delivery system will be operating more or less smoothly. Of equal importance, basic organizational norms will have been established and authority relationships negotiated.

Although this phase is free of many of the stressful problems that previously afflicted the organization, the end is still not in sight. This period of relative tranquility might be compared with having arrived in the eye of a typhoon: There is little time for complacency because a second upheaval is likely to follow. At Centerton, the hiatus of resolution existed only for a matter of months.

As was true of the early conflicts, strife was a predictable feature of the fourth period of growth. The sources of friction were plentiful. Competition for influence with the leader created problems, and other tensions reflected the unique character of the setting. At Centerton, for example, friction arose because teams differed in their attention to "housekeeping" details and because of disagreements about the "right" way to practice participative management.

Forces external to the organization can also influence the severity of intergroup and interpersonal conflict. If the new setting is tied to a parent organization, then expectations from this larger system may be important. This was certainly true at Centerton, where performance pressures from corporate headquarters exacerbated internal conflict in an already tense situation.

Other external factors, such as the availability of financial resources, may also affect the intensity of this period. If money is scarce, then intergroup rivalry is likely to be accentuated in the scramble for scarce resources.

There may be little that can be done about these exogenous forces, but the negative effects of intergroup conflict can be minimized by tools within the control of the new organization. First, techniques of conflict management discussed in the context of leadership challenges are equally relevant here. Second, organizational design mechanisms, such as open, equitable systems for allocating limited resources, can mitigate intergroup strife. Finally, collaborative decision making can play a role in dealing with the friction of this period. Its part is complex, however, and one worth considering in some depth.

Participation and Creation: Orchestrating the Role

Participation is a paradoxical matter in new organizations. Creating a new organization is stressful, and participative decision making has been recommended as a technique for combating role stress (French & Caplan, 1973). Participation can, for example, decrease role ambiguity, since involvement in the decision making process clarifies both the intended goals and the methods by which they are to be achieved. Participation can also increase actual and perceived control over one's life, which is likely to have a positive impact on physical and mental health. Finally, participation can increase the objective quality of decision making—and good decisions are of obvious importance in start-up situations.

But our earlier discussion of underbounded systems underscores a basic issue in the application of participative management. In a new setting involved in the essential task of boundary creation, participation may actually increase stress levels if the institution is unable to maintain a sense of direction.

Moreover, participation is hardly a decision making panacea. Most reviews of its contribution to organizational effectiveness support the notion that there are situations in which participation does not result in improvement, and it can even have adverse effects (see Lowin, 1968; Vroom, 1960). Participation can facilitate commitment, but it may or may not lead to high quality decisions, since the quality of a decision depends on the knowledge of participants involved in the decision making process and a poor solution, no matter how enthusiastically implemented, may be an inadequate substitute for one which is technically superior.

At Centerton, solutions to production problems often failed to materialize in group discussions. Given the technological complexity of the Centerton production process and the relative inexperience of new employees, this outcome is understandable. In fact, there were times when participation probably retarded the problem solving process. Even though technical expertise was in short supply, people with production experience frequently found themselves "outvoted" in an egalitarian but ineffective decision making process.

We noted in Chapter 3 that the original Centerton plant was intended to be a facility for producing disposable equipment: a relatively simple, labor-intensive product. But changing market conditions altered this preliminary plan, and the technology of the plasma fractionation facility was dramatically more complex than initially envisioned. This shift had profound effects on the potential role of inexperienced workers in the solution of production problems. As one manager commented:

> The basic concept that "motivated people are more productive"—no one disagrees with that. But motivated people without equipment that works are not very productive. Most of our technical problems were at a level that the operators couldn't solve; it takes a certain amount of knowledge to participate effectively.

The gains that could be realized through participation were limited by other factors as well. For example, opportunities for innovation in the fractionation process were constrained by federal design specifications intended to ensure product safety. And then there were the limitations of specialized equipment. Promising ideas may be difficult to implement because they are beyond the state of the art, because they are too expensive, or because the certification process would have been inordinately time consuming. Under these conditions, the potential advantages of group centered decision making were sharply attenuated.

This outcome is consistent with Vroom and Yetton's (1973) normative theory of decision making. They argue that the effectiveness of participation varies with the relative importance attached to quality, the need for acceptance of the decision by subordinates, and the time available for decision making. For a new organization struggling to produce a complex, flawless product under severe time pressures, unbounded participation often seems inappropriate. But, given the expectations most new employees took away from their introduction to the Quality of Work Life program, any solution not derived through a participative process was likely to be resisted.

All this is not to say that participation and involvement are incompatible with high technology. Taylor (1971), for example, found that sophisticated technology can have a favorable influence on the development of more democratic, autonomous, and responsible group activities. But technology can impose constraints that must be taken into account: A participative model can be successful in one setting—such as the Topeka plant described by Walton (1972) and Lawler (1977)—and unsuccessful in another.

This issue of participative management is further complicated by potential problems of altering a decision making style once the foundation of the institution has been constructed. It may be, for example, that autocratic style may be most appropriate at inception, and a participative style in maturity. But how is the transition to be managed? Indeed, is it possible to make radical changes once an organizational ethos has been created?

Perhaps part of the answer to these questions depends on the way the concept of participation is introduced into a new organization. If the nature of the start-up task is made clear at the outset, then the rationale for a continually increasing degree of participation is more likely to be accepted. And commonly held expectations of expanded collaboration would help keep the organization from fixing on a centralized, autocratic style of decision making.

A graduated approach need not mean postponing employee involvement until the start-up process is complete. In the earliest days, broad participation might be directed to issues such as governance policies and personnel guidelines. These matters directly affect the quality of working lives, and employees can make knowledgeable contributions toward their solutions. Later, the range of issues can be expanded in light of changing system boundary requirements and increased technical and process skills of employees. By this point in the life of a new organization we would expect wider involvement to contribute to individual satisfaction and, at the same time, to enhance organizational effectiveness.

Coming of Age: Managing the Transition to Maturity

As the new organization enters maturity, early developmental problems will have been negotiated. Principles governing the design of mature organizations apply equally well to the equilibrium period of a new setting. As we noted earlier, the bulk of research in organizational behavior has been directed toward mature organizations, and the literature is replete with prescriptions for designing these stable systems.

A new organization entering this period is, however, faced with the problem of moving from a period of intense activity to a stage of relative calm. Those who have worked long hours in the face of seemingly impossible challenges may suddenly find themselves in routine, maintenance positions. Here, the challenge is one of fine tuning an existing structure rather than creating a new one.

This dramatic change may come as a welcome relief, but it is also a mixed blessing. For those who have shared in the excitement and anguish of creation, the transition to "business as usual" may be accompanied by an emotional downswing.

For some, the physical demands of earlier periods will have taken their toll. Reaching the finish line is a sign that the time for regeneration has arrived, and it gives license to relax and recoup physical energy. Those who shared in the excitement of the utopian period now have a chance to reflect on their initial dreams and absorb the events they have witnessed. If their initial expectations have not been realized—and, given the nature of creation, they may not have been—then disappointment can result.

Many may also experience a sense of loss that the camaraderie and excitement of earlier times has passed. The intensity of this period has a narcotic quality that may be difficult to abandon, and the emergence of personal problems that have been temporarily set aside can make the transition even more difficult.

To compound these problems, the new organization may find itself suddenly limited in the rewards available to motivate its employees. In the early days, solving major problems and meeting obvious needs creates a climate of responsiveness that is difficult to sustain. At Centerton, for example, replacing vending machines with hot food was initially seen as a significant improvement. Over time, however, the effect of this change faded and dissatisfaction again surfaced. This process of raising the ante is predictable; in fact, it was quite consistent with the organization's own pressures for improved standards. But later improvements may be less dramatic than earlier ones, and the process of recalibration to reduced expectations is not easy.

Managing this process of change requires a sensitivity to these emotional dynamics and an adjustment of organizational structures to accommodate the new state. If a two-wave approach to staffing is used, then this is the time to begin the replacement process. If this technique is not employed, then those who participated in the start-up can be helped to deal with their feelings about the transition. Those who are most challenged by the task of creation may choose to move on to an environment more like that of a new setting. For those who elect to stay, time and energy must be devoted to ensure that the dynamics of this period are understood and worked through.

CONCLUSION

The developmental model described in this chapter provides a framework for understanding and guiding the process of organizational growth. Admittedly, it describes only a probable course of evolution, and it excludes events that predate the formal history of the organization. The nature of this "prehistorical period" may be significant, since organizations are never "spun from whole cloth"—or, to paraphrase Sarason, they are indeed fabricated, but the tailors are frequently unaware of the source of their material.

This "before the beginning" context defines the organization's relationship to existing institutions in such a way as to ensure conflict: For example, the missionary zeal of the new setting is juxtaposed against the traditional ideology from which it sprang (Sarason, 1972). Thus a complete understanding of organizational growth requires considerable knowledge of the unique circumstances surrounding the birth of a new setting—just as knowledge of a child's prenatal history may help to explain the course of individual development.

The utility of this model as an aid to understanding organizational creation may be affected by other unknowns. We cannot say, for example, what effect cross-level synchrony—or lack of it—may have on the course of evolution. What happens when the life cycles of individual members coincide with the life cycle of the organization? One possibility is that events are superimposed in the fashion of electronic waves, so that the impact of each is exaggerated. But this is speculative, and more systematic, empirical investigation is needed.

At the same time, the central problems of organizational creation can be stated with some confidence, and it is possible to identify a set of interventions uniquely appropriate to the beginning of the organizational life cycle. Of course, the creation of a new setting will always be accompanied by uncertainty. Unanticipated problems are inevitable and, as Michael and Mirvis (1977) observe, "There is no need to expect that, with the application of knowledge and skill, things should always turn out right" (p. 317). But a better understanding of emergent social systems can improve the likelihood that a new organization will negotiate this challenging period with purpose and competence.

Epilogue

Some five years after the Quality of Work Life program had formally ended, we returned to Centerton. Our visit was stimulated by several concerns. For one, we were anxious to see what had become of an organization and a set of ideas that we had been intensely involved with for a significant portion of our lives. Our interest extended, of course, beyond the institutional saga. We also wanted to see what had become of the individuals we had known personally—those who had shaped the Centerton experience.

A second set of questions concerned the schema we had constructed to frame the process of creation. Although our conceptualization was informed by the empirical events we observed at Centerton, we had made an effort to take an independent look at existing theoretical statements on the phenomenon of creation. The resulting integration of those perspectives was consistent with the Centerton saga. But we wanted to present the model to those who were direct participants in the process, and to pose two basic questions. First, we wanted to know if the conceptual framework fit the way in which they experienced the beginning stages of Centerton's creation. Second, we were anxious to know if the model enhanced their understanding of the start-up process; that is, if it enabled them to see familiar events in a new light, or clarified elements of the experience that had previously gone unnoticed or misunderstood.

The return visit was a stimulating and nostalgic event. We were pleased to find that many of the original employees were still at Centerton, and even more gratified to discover that most remembered us and welcomed us back. The organization had expanded substantially since our departure. Vast warehouse spaces that had been empty were now filled, and the employee population had nearly tripled. Significantly, our arrival coincided with the first time in the history of the plant that some sort of start-up was not underway—either a new foundation coming out of the ground or a new product coming on line.

Our return after a 5-year hiatus created a stroboscopic, discontinuous effect. We were struck by the sense of stability that seemed to pervade the plant. Things were far from calm, since our visit followed shortly after a tough inspection from the Food and Drug Administration. But it was obvious that the chaotic days of start-up had long since passed; Centerton was no longer an underbounded system, but, rather, an organization moving ahead with a clear sense of direction.

During our 3-day visit, we spoke with a cross-section of as many of the original employees as our time would allow. We asked a number of broad, open-ended questions. What has happened since we left? Looking back, how do you see the Quality of Work Life program—both the good and the bad? If you had it to do over again, what would you do differently? And, finally, what have you learned that might help others in the process of organizational creation?

Our interviews produced some surprises, along with corroboration of a number of our beliefs about the Centerton start-up. Most of the managers we spoke with felt that our theoretical schema reflected the early days with considerable fidelity. In two cases, people we spoke with had reservations about the distinctiveness of the second and fourth stages; that is, they questioned the independence of leader–member conflict and intergroup–interpersonal conflict.

These reservations mirrored our own. There are theoretical reasons for differentiating between the two stages, but we also found the periods to be much less distinct empirically. Thus these comments were not entirely unexpected and spoke directly to an issue that we were grappling with ourselves. What we did not predict, however, was that the Centerton managers—and particularly the Plant Manager—were nonplussed to discover that leadership crises are characteristic events in the creation of new settings. The realization that such confrontations are *de rigueur* had an unintended and apparently beneficial effect. For the younger supervisors, it placed their sometimes traumatic experiences in the larger context of the organizational life cycle. For more seasoned managers, it enabled them to step back from their experience with mature organizations and see these early power struggles from a new vantage point. Rather than focusing exclusively on the characteristics of individual actors, this perspective enabled them to see the systemic nature of leadership conflicts.

Although one cannot be sure, it seems likely that—had this understanding of the process of creation been present earlier— Centerton's leadership conflicts would have stood a much greater chance of being favorably resolved. Having a conceptual map for the events seemed to provide a mechanism for achieving some emotional distance, thereby introducing the possibility of alternative explanations for conflictual events. Thus we believe that the awareness of role demands in the process of creation could have enabled key players to move beyond personalistic attributions—and toward positions of mutual accommodations.

We also came away from our visit with a new perspective on the meaning of the Quality of Work Life intervention, both for Centerton as an organization, and for the people who embarked on the adventure. At the conclusion of the study, we were anything but sanguine about the future of the enterprise. Many employees seemed bitter and anxious to forget "PM"—participative management—perhaps even using problems with the Quality of Work Life program as an excuse to reject the fundamental concept of collaborative decision making. Others simply seemed weary, lacking the vitality to implement principles they believed in.

Certainly, there were few visible signs of the Quality of Work Life program on our return visit. Bulletin boards no longer carried news of consulting activities or the research effort, and the fervor for team meetings had subsided. It was clear that the Quality of Work Life program no longer existed as an intact entity, and that a search for a set of activities identical to those introduced by the consultants would be futile.

This situation seems common among organizations attempting behavioral science programs, and one possible explanation is that such efforts are transient phenomena with little or no chance of enduring impact. During an evening with colleagues at York University, we debated this issue at considerable length. To some, it seemed as if each movement—Organization Development, Quality of Work Life, or the next—promised little more than a new set of gimmicks that would be appropriately discarded when the opening fanfare had faded. Others disagreed, and the discussion was lively.

Our view is that the Centerton Quality of Work Life program did indeed disappear. But our interviews with the veterans of those early days uncovered evidence that it had evolved into something else: a philosophy of management consistent with the idiomatic characteristics of the organization, and a set of techniques congruent with the needs of individual managers.

We believe that the program had profound effects on Centerton employees. These effects may not have been identical with the results intended by the consultants, but they were those that survived the pragmatic demands of the workplace. As a widely respected, younger manager later reflected:

> We didn't have any idea of what supervision was meant to be . . . as it was presented to us, many felt there was no final decision by the supervisor unless they could agree like a jury by consensus of the whole group. The supervisor didn't know that he had the right to step in and say, "Okay, I hear your point, however, we have to do it this way because. . . ." We were babes out of toyland.

> What it amounts to is that no theory is best for any one person. You have to look at them all, be receptive to the ideas, and then adopt what you want. . . . To me participative management is the same thing as the golden rule . . . if you want to be told what to do all the time, then tell people what to do; if you want to be involved, then you're going to have to listen to other people.

> I don't want to spend time with someone that I feel is not going to be responsive, like a father trying to convert him; what I am saying is that I want to be able to use participative management for those who feel the same as I do . . . that's how participative management has helped me.

Comments such as these made it clear to us that the Quality of Work Life program had a significant influence on participating individuals and the character of the organization itself. This influence did not, however, take the form of a coherent set of ideas originating from external sources. It was, rather, an eclectic incorporation resulting from the collision of theoretical principles, environmental demands, technological requirements, and the prejudices and values of the individuals who created the organization.

This process of adoption and rejection was not one we had fully anticipated, and the selective incorporation made it difficult to document the institutionalization of a distinct set of behavioral science principles. But Centerton's response to the

Quality of Work Life intervention may well represent the most predictable reaction to a complex set of internal and external forces. Placed in the broader context of social evolution, this process is repeated continually as a promising innovation creates variability in human behavior; adaptive elements are selected and retained; and unworkable recipes are discarded.

Viewed macroscopically, movements such as the Quality of Work Life program can be portrayed as turbulence producing waves in the continuing evolution of social science. Proponents of such ideas may hope that their concepts will remain intact, and a certain amount of religiosity may be needed for any particular set of ideas to have substantial impact. But the transient character of any innovation should not, necessarily, be equated with failure or lack of utility. As Campbell (1975) has observed, the process of social evolution invariably reflects the wisdom of the past: It is to be expected that new concepts, having served their function, will recede as more adaptive strategies emerge.

This global perspective does not, of course, relieve social scientists of their obligation to try, to the best of their ability, to fit prescriptions to the pressing needs of organizations and individuals. The paradigm of social evolution is unlikely to console members of an organization who have attempted unworkable ideas or who have been led to expect results that do not occur. But the conceptualization, and the history of behavioral science, do have implications for the way in which innovations are introduced into organizational settings. Rather than presenting promising ideas as immutable scientific principles, it makes prudent and ethical sense to make sure that practitioners understand their role in testing the robustness of theoretical prescriptions—however valid these concepts may be to their creators and proponents.

This testing process was, for many at Centerton, a painful experience. But veterans of the Quality of Work Life program are now sophisticated consumers of managerial innovation, and it appears that their expertise may be put to immediate use. At the end of our visit we discovered that corporate headquarters had recently endorsed a new concept called "quality circles." Apparently unaware of their earlier position on participative management, Crown management was encouraging Centerton to involve employees in quality circles to improve the production of disposable equipment—the product for which the Quality of Work Life program was initially designed.

Of course, quality circles are not the same as Quality of Work Life. As currently planned, the new concept will incorporate some of the structural features that were previously lacking, and involvement will take place around a simple production process amenable to broad participation. But it seems certain that veterans of the Centerton start-up will subject the new program to considerable scrutiny. They are no longer babes in utopia.

References

Alderfer, C. P. (1972) Existence, relatedness, and growth. New York: The Free Press.

Alderfer, C. P. (1976) *Change processes in organizations.* In M. D. Dunnette (Ed.), *Handbook of industrial and organizational psychology.* Chicago: Rand-McNally.

Alderfer, C. P. (1979) Consulting to underbounded systems. In C. P. Alderfer & C. L. Cooper (Eds.), *Advances in experiential social processes* (Vol. 2). New York: Wiley.

Alferfer, C. P., & Berg, D. N. (1977) Organizational development: The profession and the practitioner. In P. H. Mirvis & D. N. Berg (Eds.), *Failures in organization development and change: Cases and essays for learning.* New York: Wiley.

Argyris, C. (1970) *Intervention theory and method: A behavioral science view.* Reading, MA: Addison-Wesley.

Aronson, E., & Mills, J. (1959) The effect of severity of initiation on liking for a group. *Journal of Abnormal and Social Psychology,* **59**, 177–181.

Barnes, L. B. (1971) Organizational change and field experiment methods. In J. D. Thompson & V. H. Vroom (Eds.), *Organizational design and research.* Pittsburgh: University of Pittsburgh Press.

Bem, D. J. (1967) Self-perception: The dependent variable of human performance. *Organizational Behavior and Human Performance,* **2**, 105–121.

Bennis, W. G. (1966) *Changing organizations.* New York: McGraw-Hill.

Bennis, W. G., & Shepard, H. A. (1974) A theory of group development. In G. Gibbard, J. J. Hartman, & R. D. Mann (Eds.), *Analysis of groups.* San Francisco: Jossey-Bass.

265

Berg, D. N. (1977) Failure at entry. In P. H. Mirvis & D. N. Berg (Eds.), *Failures in organization development and change: Cases and essays for learning.* New York: Wiley-Interscience.

Bertalanffy, L. V. (1968) *General system theory.* New York: Braziller.

Bierbrauer, G. A. (1973) *Attribution and perspective: Effects of time set and role on interpersonal inference.* Unpublished doctoral dissertation, Stanford University.

Bion, W. R. (1959) *Experiences in groups.* London: Tavistock.

Blalock, H. M. (1964) *Causal inferences in nonexperimental research.* New York: Norton.

Brayfield, A. H., & Crockett, W. H. (1955) Employee attitudes and employee performance. *Psychological Bulletin,* **52,** 396–424.

Campbell, D. T. (1963) From description to experimentation: Interpreting trends as quasi-experiments. In C. W. Harris (Ed.), *Problems in measuring change.* Madison, WI: University of Wisconsin Press.

Campbell, D. T. (1971) *Methods for the experimenting society.* Preliminary draft of a paper presented at a meeting of the Eastern Psychological Association, Washington, D.C., April.

Campbell, D. T. (1975) On the conflicts between biological and social evolution and between psychology and moral tradition. *American Psychologist,* **30** (12), 1103–1126.

Campbell, D. T., & Stanley, J. C. (1963) *Experimental and quasi-experimental designs for research.* Chicago: Rand McNally.

Caporaso, J. A., & Roos, L. L. (Eds.) (1973) *Quasi-experimental approaches: Testing theory and evaluating policy.* Evanston, IL: Northwestern University Press.

Charters, W. E., & Jones, J. E. (1973) On the risk of appraising non-events in program evaluation. *Evaluation Researcher,* **11,** 5–7.

Cook, T. D., & Campbell, D. T. (1975) The design and conduct of quasi-experiments and true experiments in field settings. In M. D. Dunnette (Ed.), *Handbook of industrial and organizational psychology.* Chicago: Rand McNally.

Cronbach, L. J., & Furby, L. (1970) How should we measure change—Or should we? *Psychological Bulletin,* **74** (1), 68–80.

Davidson, T. N. (1972) *Youth in transition: Evaluation of a strategy for longitudinal analysis of survey panel data* (Vol. 4). Ann Arbor, MI: Institute for Social Research.

Davis, L. E., & Sullivan, C. S. (1980) A labour-management contract and quality of working life. *Journal of Occupational Behavior,* **1,** 29–42.

de Charms, R. (1968) *Personal causation.* New York: Academic Press.

Erikson, E. H. (1963) *Childhood and society* (2nd ed.). New York: Norton.

Erikson, E. H. (1968) *Identity, youth, and crisis.* New York: Norton.

Festinger, L. (1957). *A theory of cognitive dissonance.* Stanford, CA: Stanford University Press.

Filley, A. C. (1975) *Interpersonal conflict resolution.* Dallas: Scott, Foresman.

Flavell, J. H. (1963) *The developmental psychology of Jean Piaget.* New York: Van Nostrand.

Fleishman, E. A. (1953) Leadership climate, human relations training and supervisory behavior. *Personnel Psychology,* **6,** 205–222.

Freeman, H. E., & Sherwood, C. C. (1965) Research in large scale intervention programs. *Journal of Social Issues,* **21** (1), 11–28.

French, J. R. P., Jr. (1973) Person role fit. *Occupational Mental Health,* **3** (1), 15–20.

French, J. R. P., Jr., & Caplan, R. D. (1973) Organizational stress and individual strain. In A. J. Marrow (Ed.), *The failure of success.* New York: AMACOM.

Ginsberg, H., & Opper, S. (1969) *Piaget's theory of intellectual development.* Englewood Cliffs, NJ: Prentice-Hall.

Glaser, E. M. (1976) *Productivity gains through worklife improvement.* New York: Psychological Corporation.

Glaser, E. M., & Backer, T. E. (1972) A clinical approach to program evaluation. *Evaluation,* 54–59.

Glaser, B. G., & Strauss, A. L. (1967) *The discovery of grounded theory: Strategies for qualitative research.* Chicago: Aldine.

Gold, R. L. (1970) Roles in sociological field observations. In N. K. Denzin (Ed.), *Sociological methods: A sourcebook.* Chicago: Aldine.

Goldenberg, I. I. (1971) *Build me a mountain: Youth, poverty, and the creation of new settings.* Cambridge, MA: MIT Press.

Gould, S. J. (1980) Sociobiology and the theory of natural selection. In G. W. Barlow & J. Silverberg (Eds.), *Sociobiology: Beyond nature/nurture?* Washington, DC: Westview for the American Academy of Arts and Sciences.

Greiner, L. E. (1970) Patterns of organizational change. In G. Dalton & P. R. Lawrence (Eds.), *Organizational change and development.* Georgetown, Ontario: Irwin-Doresey, Ltd.

Greiner, L. E. (1972) Evolution and revolution as organizations grow. *Harvard Business Review,* **50,** 37–46.

Guttentag, M., & Struening, E. L. (1975) The handbook: Its purpose and organization. In M. Guttentag & E. L. Struening (Eds.), *Handbook of evaluation research* (Vol. 2). Beverly Hills: Sage.

Hackman, J. R., & Lawler, E. E. (1971) Employee reactions to job characteristics. *Journal of Applied Psychology,* **55** (3), 259–286.

Hackman, J. R., & Oldham, G. (1974) A new strategy for job enrichment. *Administrative Sciences Technical Report*, May 3.

Hartman, J. J., & Gibbard, G. S. (1974a) A note on fantasy themes in the evolution of group culture. In G. Gibbard, J. J. Hartman, & R. D. Mann (Eds.), *Analysis of groups*. San Francisco: Jossey-Bass.

Hartman, J. J., & Gibbard, G. S. (1974b) Anxiety, boundary evolution, and social change. In G. Gibbard, J. J. Hartman, & R. D. Mann (Eds.), *Analysis of groups*. San Francisco: Jossey-Bass.

Heller, K., & Monahan, J. (1977) *Psychology and community change*. Homewood, IL: Dorsey.

Herzberg, F. (1966) *Work and the nature of man*. Cleveland: World.

Hill, W. R., & Gruner, L. (1973) A Study of development in open and closed groups. *Small group behavior*, **4**, 355–381.

Holmes, T. H., & Rahe, R. H. (1967) The social readjustment scale. *Journal of Psychosomatic Research*, **11**, 213–218.

House, J. S., & Wells, J. A. (1978) Occupational stress, social support, and health. In A. McLean, G. Black, & M. Colligan (Eds.), *Reducing occupational stress*. U.S. Department of Health, Education and Welfare.

Hummel-Rossi, B., & Weinberg, S. L. (1975) Practical guidelines in applying current theories to the measurement of change. *JSAS Catalog of Selected Documents in Psychology*, **5**, 226.

Janis, I., & Mann, L. (1977) *Decision-making*. New York: Free Press.

Janis, I., & Wheeler, D. (1978) Thinking clearly about career choices. *Psychology Today*, May.

Jenkins, G. D., & Lawler, E. E. (1981) Impact of employee participation in development of a pay plan. *Organizational Behavior and Human Performance*, **28**, 111–128.

Jenkins, G. D., Nadler, D. A., Lawler, E. E., & Cammann, C. (1975) Standardized observations: An approach to measuring the nature of jobs. *Journal of Applied Psychology*, **60**, 171–181.

Jones, E. E., & Nisbett, R. E. (1972) The actor and the observer: Divergent perceptions of the causes of behavior. In E. E. Jones, D. E. Kanouse, & H. H. Kelley (Eds.), *Attribution: Perceiving the causes of behavior*. Morristown, NJ: General Learning Press.

Junker, B. H. (1960) *Field work: An introduction to the social sciences*. Chicago: University of Chicago Press.

Kahn, R. L. (1973) Conflict, ambiguity, and overload: Three elements in job stress. *Occupational Mental Health*, **3** (1), 2–9.

Katz, D., & Kahn, R. L. (1966) *The social psychology of organizations*. New York: Wiley.

Katzel, R. A., & Yankelovich, D. (1975) *Work, productivity, and job satisfaction*. New York: The Psychological Corporation.

Kenny, D. A. (1975) A quasi-experimental approach to assessing treatment effects in the non-equivalent control group design. *Psychological Bulletin*, **82** (3), 345–362.

Kimberly, J. R. (1980) Initiation, innovation, and institutionalization in the creation process. In J. R. Kimberly & R. H. Miles (Eds.), *The organizational life cycle: Issues in the creation, transformation, and decline of organizations*. San Francisco: Jossey-Bass.

Kimberly, J. R., Miles, R. H., et al. (1980) *The organizational life cycle: Issues in the creation, transformation, and decline of organizations*. San Francisco: Jossey-Bass.

Kiresuk, T. J., & Sherman, R. E. (1968) Goal attainment scaling: A general method for evaluating comprehensive community mental health programs. *Community Mental Health Journal*, **4**, 443–453.

Lawler, E. E. (1973) Motivation in work organizations. Belmont, CA: Wadsworth.

Lawler, E. E. (1977) Adaptive experiments: An approach to organizational behavior research. *Academy of Management Review*, **2**, 576–585.

Lawler, E. E., & Porter, L. W. (1967) The effect of performance on job satisfaction. *Industrial Relations*, **7**, 20–28.

Lawler, E. E., Nadler, D. A., & Cammann, C. (1980) *Organizational assessment: Perspectives on the measurement of organizational behavior and the quality of work life*. New York: Wiley.

Likert, R. (1967) *The human organization*. New York: McGraw-Hill.

Lord, F. M., (1967) Elementary models for measuring change. In C. W. Harris (Ed.), *Problems in measuring change*. Madison, WI: University of Wisconsin Press.

Lowin, A. (1968) Participative decision making: A model, literature critique, and prescriptions for research. *Organizational Behavior and Human Performance*, **3**, 68–106.

Lowin, A., & Craig, J. R. (1968) The influence of level of performance on managerial style: An experimental object-lesson in the ambiguity of correlational data. *Organizational Behavior and Human Performance*, **3**, 440–458.

Maccoby, E. E., & Jacklin, C. N. (1974) *The psychology of sex differences*. Stanford: Stanford University Press.

McClelland, D. C. (1961) *The achieving society*. Princeton: Van Nostrand.

McGregor, D. (1960) *The human side of enterprise*. New York: McGraw-Hill.

McNemar, Q. (1969) *Psychological statistics*. New York: Wiley.

Michael, D. N., & Mirvis, P. H. (1977) Changing, erroring, and learning. In P. H. Mirvis & D. N. Berg (Eds.), *Failures in organization development and change: Cases and essays for learning*. New York: Wiley-Interscience.

Michigan organizational assessment package: Progress report II. (1975) Ann

Arbor, MI: Institute for Social Research.

Miles, R. E. (1965) Human relations or human resources? *Harvard Business Review*, **43** (4), 148–156.

Miller, J. G. (1965) Living systems: Basic concepts, structure and process, cross-level hypotheses. *Behavioral Science*, **10**, 193–237, 337–379, 380–441.

Miller, J. G. (1978) *Living systems*. New York: McGraw-Hill.

Morrison, D. E., & Henkel, R. E. (1970) *The significance test controversy*. Chicago: Aldine.

Nieva, V. F., & Perkins, D. N. T. (1980) The organizational assessment role: issues and dilemmas. In E. E. Lawler, D. A. Nadler, and C. C. Cammann (Eds.), *Organizational assessment: Perspectives on the measurement of organizational behavior and the quality of work life*. New York: Wiley.

Nieva, V. F., Perkins, D. N. T., & Lawler, E. E. (1978) Improving the quality of life at work: An evaluation of the Centerton experience (Final report to the U.S. Department of Labor, Grant No. 21-26-74-16). Ann Arbor MI: Institute for Social Research, The University of Michigan.

Nieva, V. F., Perkins, D. N. T., & Lawler, E. E. (1980) Improving the quality of life at work: Assessment of a collaborative selection process. *Journal of Occupational Behavior*, **1**, 43–52.

Pelz, D. C. & Andrews, F. M. (1964) Detecting causal priorities in panel study data. *American Sociological Review*, **29**, 836–848.

Perkins, D. N. T., Nieva, V. F., & Lawler, E. E. (1978) *Causal forces in the creation of a new organization*. (Final report to the U.S. Department of Labor, Grant No. 21-26-74-16). Ann Arbor, MI: Institute for Social Research, The University of Michigan.

Porter, L. W., Lawler, E. E., & Hackman, J. R. (1975) *Behavior in organizations*. New York: McGraw-Hill.

Porter, L. W., & Steers, R. M. (1978) Organizational, work, and personal factors in employee turnover and absenteeism. *Psychological Bulletin*, 1973, **80**, 151–176.

Poza, E. J., & Markus, M. L. (1980) Success story: The team approach to work restructuring. *Organizational Dynamics*, **9** (1), 3–25.

Rappaport, J. (1977) *Community psychology*. New York: Holt, Rinehart & Winston.

Robinson, J. P., & Shaver, P. R. (1973) *Measures of social psychological attitudes*. Ann Arbor: Survey Research Center, Institute for Social Research.

Rogosa, D. (1980) A critique of cross-lagged correlation. *Psychological Bulletin*, **2**, 245–258.

Rosenzweig, S. (1945) The picture-association method and its application in a study of reactions to frustration. *Journal of Personality*, **14**, 3–23.

Sarason, S. B. (1972) *The creation of settings and the future societies.* San Francisco: Jossey-Bass.

Seashore, S. E., & Bowers, D. G. (1963) *Changing the structure and functioning of an organization.* Ann Arbor, MI: Survey Research Center, Institute for Social Research.

Seligman, M. E. P. (1975) *Helplessness.* San Francisco: Freeman.

Sieber, S. D. (1973) The integration of fieldwork and survey methods. *American Journal of Sociology,* **78**, 1335–1359.

Singer, J. (1974) Participative decision making about work: An overdue look at variables which mediate its effects. *Sociology of Work and Occupations,* **1** (4), 347–371.

Slater, P. E. (1966) *Microcosm.* New York: Wiley.

Sproull, L., Weiner, S., & Wolf, D. (1978) *Organizing an anarchy: Belief, bureaucracy and politics in the National Institute of Education.* Chicago: University of Chicago Press.

Strauss, G. (1963) Some notes on power equalization. In H. J. Lewitt (Ed.), *The social science of organization.* Englewood Cliffs, NJ: Prentice-Hall.

Suchman, E. A. (1967) *Evaluative research: Principles and practice in public service and social action programs.* New York: Russell Sage.

Suttle, J. L. (1977) Improving life at work—Problems and prospects. In J. R. Hackman and J. L. Suttle (Eds.) *Improving life at work: Behavioral science approaches to organizational change.* Santa Monica, CA: Goodyear.

Tannenbaum, A. S. (1966) *Social psychology of the work organization.* Belmont, CA: Wadsworth.

Tannenbaum, R., & Schmidt, W. H. (1973) How to choose a leadership pattern. *Harvard Business Review,* (May–June), 162–180.

Taylor, J. C. (1971) Some effects of technology on organizational change. *Human Relations,* **24**, 105–123.

Taylor, J. C. (1973) *Concepts and problems in studies of the quality of working life.* Los Angeles: UCLA, Graduate School of Management.

Thurstone, L. L., & Jeffrey, T. E. (1959) *Closure flexibility: Concealed figures: Test administration manual.* Chicago: Educational Industry Service.

Tucker, L., Damarin, F., & Messick, S. (1966) A base-free measure of change. *Psychometrika,* **31** (4), 457–473.

Turner, A. N., & Lawrence, P. R. (1965) *Industrial jobs and the worker: An investigation of response to task attributes.* Boston: Harvard University Press.

Vroom, V. H. (1960) *Some personality determinants of the effects of participation.* Englewood Cliffs, NJ: Prentice-Hall.

Vroom, V. H. (1964) *Work and motivation.* New York: Wiley.

Vroom, V. H., & Yetton, P. H. (1973) *Leadership and decision-making*. Pittsburgh: University of Pittsburgh Press.

Walton, R. E. (1969) *Interpersonal peacemaking: Confrontations and third party consultation*. Reading, MA: Addison-Wesley.

Walton, R. E. (1972) How to counter alienation in the plant. *Harvard Business Review*, **50**, 70–81.

Walton, R. E. (1979) Improving the quality of life at work. *Harvard Business Review*, May–June, pp. 12ff.

Walton, R. E., & Schlesinger, L. A. (1979) Do supervisors thrive in participative work systems? *Organizational Dynamics*, **8** (3), 25–38.

Wanous, J. P. (1978) A job preview makes recruiting more effective. *Harvard Business Review*, **53** (16), 166–168.

Wanous, J. P. (1977) Organizational entry: The individual's viewpoint. In J. R. Hackman, E. E. Lawler, & L. W. Porter (Eds.), *Perspectives on behavior in organizations*, New York: McGraw-Hill.

Webb, E. J., Campbell, D. T., Schwartz, R. D., & Sechrest, L. (1966) *Unobtrusive measures: Non-reactive research in the social sciences*. Chicago: Rand-McNally.

Weiss, C. H. (1972) *Evaluation research: Methods for assessing program effectiveness*. Englewood Cliffs, NJ: Prentice-Hall.

White, R. W. (1959) Motivation reconsidered: The concept of competence. *Psychological Review*, **66**, 297–333.

Winch, R. F., & Campbell, D. T. (1970) *Proof? No. Evidence? Yes: The significance of test controversy*. Chicago: Aldine.

Work in America. (1973) Report of a special task force to the Secretary of Health, Education, and Welfare. Cambridge, MA: MIT Press.

Wortman, C. B. (1976) Causal attributions and personal control. In J. Ickes & R. F. Kidd (Eds.), *New Directions in Attribution Research* (Vol. 1). Hillsdale, NJ: Lawrence Erlbaum.

Yukl, G. (1971) Toward a behavioral theory of leadership. *Organizational Behavior and Human Performance*, **6** (4), 414–440.

Author Index

Alderfer, C. P., 18, 171, 238
Andrews, F. M., 138
Argyris, C., 178, 238
Aronson, E., 242

Backer, T. C., 127, 130
Barnes, L. B., 115
Bem, D. J., 242
Bennis, W. G., 21, 25, 26, 31,
  60
Berg, D. N., 138
Bertalanffy, L. V., 35
Bierbrauer, G. A., 218
Bion, W. R., 21, 33
Blalock, H. M., 139
Bowers, D. G., 141
Brayfield, A. H., 169

Cammann, C., 115, 234
Campbell, D. T., 117, 131, 134,
  135, 137, 138, 140, 141, 142,
  168, 193, 262.
Caplan, R. D., 249
Caporoso, J. A., 117
Charters, W. E., 116
Cook, T. D., 137, 138, 141
Craig, J. R., 232
Crockett, W. H., 169
Cronback, L. J., 136

Damarin, F., 136

Davidson, T. N., 136
Davis, L. E., 5
deCharms, R., 243

Erickson, E. H., 22, 27, 30,
  37

Festinger, L., 242, 243
Filley, A. C., 247
Flavell, J. H., 36
Fleishman, E. A., 215
Freeman, H. E., 116
French, J. R. P., 241, 249
Furby, L., 136

Gibbard, G. S., 20, 21, 25, 26,
  29, 31, 32
Ginsberg, H., 36
Glaser, B. G., 117, 127
Glaser, E. M., 127, 130,
  185
Gold, R. L., 130
Goldenberg, I. I., 23, 24, 28,
  29, 245, 246
Gould, S. J., 38
Greiner, L. E., 20, 24, 26, 27,
  31, 144
Gruner, L., 19
Guttentag, M., 126

Hackman, J. R., 58, 162, 242

Subject Index

277